WILD EDIBLE PLANTS OF CALIFORNIA

LOCATE, IDENTIFY, STORE, AND PREPARE YOUR FORAGED FINDS

FORAGE AND FEAST SERIES: COMPREHENSIVE GUIDES TO FORAGING ACROSS AMERICA

BOOK 2

SHANNON WARNER

Rowan's

PUBLISHING

ALSO BY SHANNON WARNER

<u>**Individual Regions:**</u>
Wild Edible Plants of the Mid-Atlantic
Wild Edible Plants of New England
Wild Edible Plants of the Southwest
Wild Edible Plants of the Pacific Northwest
Wild Edible Plants of Texas
Wild Edible Plants of the Great Lakes *(Coming Soon)*
Wild Edible Plants of the Great Plains *(Coming Soon)*
Wild Edible Plants of the Southeast *(Coming Soon)*
Wild Edible Plants of the Gulf Coast *(Coming Soon)*
Wild Edible Plants of the Upper Midwest *(Coming Soon)*
Wild Edible Plants of the Rocky Mountains *(Coming Soon)*

<u>**2-in-1 Guides:**</u>
Wild Edibles of the West Coast (California & the Pacific Northwest)
Wild Edibles of the Northeast (Mid-Atlantic & New England)
Foraging the Wild South (Texas & the Southwest)
Foraging the Midwest *(Coming Soon)*
Foraging the Southeast *(Coming Soon)*
Foraging the North *(Coming Soon)*

INTRODUCTION

California is abundant, with a diverse range of landscapes, including towering forests, expansive deserts, and pristine coastlines. This rich and varied environment is home to an incredible array of plant species, many of which are not only beautiful but also delicious and nutritious.

Throughout history, the people of California have depended on wild plants for their sustenance, using them in a wide range of traditional recipes and medicinal preparations. Wild plants have played an important role in this land's cultural and culinary traditions, from the region's indigenous peoples to the Spanish colonizers who arrived in the 18th century. Today, interest in wild edible plants is increasing, driven by a desire for healthier, more sustainable, and more diverse food sources. As more and more people seek out locally grown and foraged foods, wild edible plants are increasingly recognized as valuable and delicious additions to our diets. Wild edible plants offer a host of nutritional benefits, including vitamins, minerals, fiber, and antioxidants. These benefits can help support overall health and wellness and may even protect against chronic diseases like heart disease, cancer, and diabetes.

This book is a comprehensive guide to California's many wild edible plants. We will explore the nutritional benefits, traditional uses, and culinary potential of a wide range of wild plants and provide tips and guidelines for foraging safely and sustainably.

As we delve into the world of wild edible plants, we will discover a wealth of flavors and textures that are sure to delight the palate. However, it is essential to approach wild edible plants with caution and respect. Some plants can be toxic or cause allergic reactions, and it is necessary to correctly identify and prepare any wild edible plants before consuming them. Foraging should also be done sustainably, preserving the health of the environment and the plants themselves.

This book celebrates the rich and diverse plant life that thrives throughout California. Whether you are a seasoned forager or simply curious about the many wild edible plants that can be found in your own backyard, we hope that this book will serve as a valuable and informative guide to the world of wild food in California.

HARVESTING RESPONSIBLY
PRACTICES FOR ETHICAL AND SUSTAINABLE GATHERING

Foraging is a popular activity in California, and for a good reason. The state is home to a diverse array of wild plants, mushrooms, and seaweeds, many of which are delicious and highly nutritious. However, it's essential to forage ethically and responsibly to preserve the health of the environment and the plants.

It is important to follow a few guidelines to forage ethically and responsibly. First and foremost, always obtain permission before foraging on private property, and be mindful of any regulations or restrictions that may be in place in certain areas.

Foraging can have a positive impact on the environment when it is done ethically and sustainably. By foraging in a way that does not harm the environment or the plants themselves, we can help preserve California's natural beauty and promote a healthy and diverse ecosystem.

Many of California's wild plants are threatened by over-harvesting and habitat destruction. As more people become interested in foraging, there is a risk that popular plants may be over-harvested, and their populations may decline. This will cause a ripple effect on the entire ecosystem, as other plants and animals that depend on those plants for food and shelter will also be impacted. So take only what you need and don't take more than the plant can sustainably provide. For example, if you come across a patch of wild berries, it is important to take only what you can eat or preserve and leave some for other foragers and the animals that depend on those berries for food.

Another reason foraging ethically is so important is that indigenous communities use many wild plants in California for traditional and cultural purposes. These plants have been essential to indigenous cultures for thousands of years, and their traditional uses should be respected and honored.

Finally, it is essential to dispose of any waste properly and to leave the area better than you found it. This includes packing out trash or debris and avoiding actions that could harm the environment or the plants.

Foraging ethically and responsibly is essential in California, both to protect the health of the environment and the plants themselves and to respect the traditional and cultural uses of these plants by indigenous communities. Following a few simple guidelines and approaching foraging with respect and responsibility can help preserve California's natural beauty and promote a thriving and diverse ecosystem.

STARTING YOUR FORAGING JOURNEY

Foraging for wild plants is a rewarding and enjoyable activity that can provide fresh, delicious, and nutritious ingredients for your cooking. However, it is important to approach foraging with the right mindset and knowledge to do it safely and successfully. Here are some tips to help you successfully forage for wild plants:

Do Your Research: Before setting out, it is important to research the plants that you are looking for. This includes learning how to correctly identify them and their nutritional and medicinal properties.

Plan Your Route: Once you have identified the plants you want to forage, plan your route carefully. Research where you will be foraging, and ensure you have permission to be there if necessary. Bringing a map or GPS device to help you navigate is also a good idea.

Bring the Right Tools: Foraging requires some basic tools to help you identify and harvest the plants you seek.

Here are some tools that can be useful when harvesting foraged wild plants:

- A reliable field guide or plant identification app can help you identify the plants you are foraging and determine the best way to harvest them.

- A sharp knife or scissors can be used to carefully cut leaves, stems, and other parts of the plant without damaging the surrounding area or other parts of the plant.

- Pruning shears can help make clean cuts and help preserve woodier plants with thicker stems.

- Gloves protect your hands from thorns, prickly leaves, or harmful plants.

- A sturdy basket or bag to collect and transport harvested plants. Avoid using plastic bags as they can trap moisture and promote spoilage.

Please respect the Environment: When foraging, it is important to respect the environment and the plants themselves. Only take what you need; never take over one-third of any plant. Avoid trampling or damaging the surrounding area, and try not to disturb any wildlife or other natural resources.

Harvest Responsibly: When harvesting, take care only to collect healthy specimens that are free from disease or pests. If you are unsure whether a plant is safe to eat, err on the side of caution and don't harvest it. Also, properly identify the plant and its parts before harvesting, as some plants have toxic or inedible parts.

Clean and Store Your Harvest: Once you have harvested your plants, cleaning and storing them correctly is important. Rinse them in cool water to remove dirt or debris, and pat them dry with a clean towel. Store them in a cool, dry place until you can use them.

Cook and Enjoy: It is time to cook and enjoy your wild plants. Many delicious and nutritious recipes can be made with foraged ingredients, including salads, soups, stews, and more. Just be sure to cook or prepare the plants properly before eating, and always follow food safety guidelines.

Foraging for wild plants can be a fun and rewarding activity, but it requires knowledge, respect, and responsibility. By following these tips, you can successfully forage wild plants and enjoy nature's delicious and nutritious ingredients.

Now, let us walk across the state and learn about the vast areas we will explore.

PART ONE
FROM THE MOUNTAINS TO THE COASTLINE

EXPLORING THE DIVERSE REGIONS OF CALIFORNIA

CHAPTER 1
NORTHERN CALIFORNIA

Northern California is a region that spans from the San Francisco Bay Area to the Oregon border. It is known for its stunning natural beauty, diverse landscapes, and mild climate.

- It has many elevations, from sea level along the coast to towering mountain peaks in the Sierra Nevada range. The highest peak in the region is Mount Shasta, which stands at 14,179 feet above sea level.
- It experiences a Mediterranean climate with mild, wet winters and warm, dry summers. The temperature can vary significantly depending on elevation and proximity to the coast. Along the coast, temperatures typically range from 50 to 70 degrees Fahrenheit throughout the year. Inland, temperatures can vary from 70 to 100 degrees Fahrenheit in the summer and 30 to 50 degrees Fahrenheit in the winter.
- It has distinct seasons, with spring and fall being the mildest and most pleasant. Summers can be hot and dry, while winters can be wet and chilly. Fall is a popular time for foraging, as many edible plants and fungi are abundant during this season.

Northern California is a hotbed of wild foods, with an abundance of mushrooms, seaweeds, wildflowers, and berries.

- ISO RABINS, FOUNDER OF FORAGESF

Northern California is a forager's paradise, with diverse edible plants, fungi, and seafood. Some of the best places to forage in the region include:

- **Point Reyes National Seashore:** This park is home to various edible plants, including seaweed, berries, and mushrooms.

- **Mendocino County:** This region is famous for its wild mushrooms, including chanterelles and morels.
- **Napa Valley:** This area is known for its wild grapes and blackberries, found along hiking trails and vineyards.
- **Sierra Nevada Mountains:** The high elevations of the Sierra Nevada range are home to various edible plants and mushrooms, including huckleberries, wild onions, and pine nuts.

There are several foraging groups in Northern California, which can be an excellent resource for those looking to learn more about local edible plants and fungi.

Some popular foraging groups in the area include:

- **ForageSF** organizes foraging walks and events throughout the San Francisco Bay Area. https://www.foragesf.com/
- **Humboldt Mycological Society** focuses on identification, ecology, photography, and more. It is a group whose interest is in the fungi found in northwestern California. Conduct monthly informative meetings, field trips, workshops, and annual Mushroom trips. More information: http://hbmycologicalsociety.org/wp/
- **Mycological Society of San Francisco** was created to enhance people's understanding and enjoyment of mushrooms and fungi. Every year, they sponsor classes that discuss mushroom identification, cultivation, basics of mycology, and more. More information: http://www.mssf.org/index.html
- **HarvestWild:** Formerly known as The Northern California Guide, offers guided tours for hunting, fishing, and gathering as well as a Field to Table food prep class. More information: https://www.harvestwild.com/
- **Sierra Botanica:** Rachel and Matt Berry, and Amara are the people behind Sierra Botanica, located in Northern California. They want to promote health and wellness in a multi-disciplinary, holistic form. Offers herbalism classes. More information: http://sierrabotanica.com/about/

CHAPTER 2
CENTRAL CALIFORNIA

Central California is a region that spans from the San Francisco Bay Area to Santa Barbara County. It is known for its fertile agricultural land, scenic coastline, and diverse landscapes.

- It's a region of varied elevations. The area includes the coastal mountains, with heights up to 5,000 feet, and the Central Valley, located at approximately sea level.
- It has a semi-arid climate with hot, dry summers and mild, wet winters. Temperatures can vary greatly depending on elevation, with coastal temperatures ranging from the mid-50s to mid-70s and inland temperatures reaching up to 100 degrees Fahrenheit in the summer.
- It experiences distinct seasons. Spring and fall are generally mild and pleasant, while summers are hot and dry. Winters are often rainy, with occasional frost and fog.

Surely the Lord will not refuse one who is so eager to behold and learn. And so, with a light heart and an ever-growing joy, I pushed on into the Great Central Plain of California.

-JOHN MUIR, THE FAMOUS NATURALIST AND CONSERVATIONIST

Central California has diverse edible plants, fungi, and seafood to forage. Some of the best places to forage in the area include:

- **Big Sur:** This region is known for its abundant wildflowers, berries, and seaweed.

- **Pinnacles National Park:** This park has various edible plants and mushrooms, including manzanita berries and chanterelles.
- **Los Padres National Forest:** This area is known for its edible mushrooms, such as chanterelles and morels.
- **Santa Barbara Channel:** The Santa Barbara Channel provides a variety of edible seaweed and shellfish, including mussels and sea urchins.

Foraging groups in Central California provide education and resources for foragers. Some popular foraging groups in the region include:

- **Central Coast Wilds** is dedicated to exploring the wild foods of the Central Coast, including edible plants, seaweed, and shellfish. More information: http://www.centralcoastwilds.com/
- **Fungus Federation of Santa Cruz** focuses on exploring and identifying wild mushrooms in the Santa Cruz region. More Information: https://ffsc.us/

CHAPTER 3
COASTAL CALIFORNIA

Coastal California is a region that stretches along the Pacific Ocean from the northern border of the state to the southern border. It is known for its breath-taking natural beauty and abundant wildlife.

- The elevation along the coast varies significantly, with sea level along the shoreline and mountains rising to over 14,000 feet inland. The coastal mountains provide a dramatic backdrop for the region's stunning beaches and coastal ecosystems.
- It enjoys a mild, Mediterranean climate with warm, dry summers and cool, wet winters. The average temperature in coastal California is around 60 degrees Fahrenheit, with high temperatures averaging in the mid-70s in the summer and lows in the mid-40s in the winter.
- It has distinct seasons, with spring and fall being the mildest and most pleasant. Summers are warm and dry, with foggy mornings and cooler temperatures along the coast. Winter is the wettest season, with occasional heavy rains and cooler temperatures.

There is an edible landscape in California - the slopes of the mountains, the beaches, the deserts - that is a delicious revelation to anyone who will walk the land with an open heart.

-ALICE WATERS, RENOWNED CHEF AND FOOD ACTIVIST

Coastal California is home to various edible plants, fungi, and seafood. Some of the best places to forage in the area include:

- **Marin Headlands:** This park has various edible plants, including seaweed, berries, and mushrooms.

- **Point Lobos State Natural Reserve:** This area is known for its large kelp beds, which provide a source of edible seaweed.
- **Santa Cruz Mountains:** This region is famous for its wild mushrooms, including chanterelles and morels.
- **Sonoma Coast State Park:** This area is home to various edible plants, including sea rockets, sea lettuce, and wild fennel.

Foraging groups provide a wealth of knowledge and resources to foragers in the area. Some of the most popular foraging groups include:

- **North Coast Harvesters** is focused on exploring the edible plants, fungi, and seafood of the North Coast region. More information: https://www.facebook.com/groups/533815677224056/
- **Mendocino Coast Mushroom Club** comprises local fungi foragers in Fort Bragg, California. The group finds wild mushrooms, identifies them, cooks, and more. Hosts forays, workshops, meetings, and guest speakers.
- More information: https://www.mendocinocoastmushroomclub.org/

CHAPTER 4
SOUTHERN CALIFORNIA

S outhern California is a region that spans from Santa Barbara County to the Mexican border. It is known for its warm, sunny climate, beautiful beaches, and vibrant cities.

- Its a region of varied elevations, ranging from sea level along the coast to over 10,000 feet in the San Bernardino Mountains.
- It has a Mediterranean climate with warm, dry summers and mild, wet winters. The average temperature in coastal Southern California is around 70 degrees Fahrenheit, with high temperatures averaging in the mid-80s in the summer and lows in the mid-50s in the winter.
- It has mild seasons, with spring and fall being the most pleasant. Summers can be sweltering and dry, with occasional heat waves, while winters are generally mild, with infrequent rains.

I often think that Southern California is a garden of earthly delights, where the terrain and climate conspire to bring forth a dizzying array of foods.

- RUSS PARSONS, FOOD WRITER AND AUTHOR

It has a variety of edible plants, fungi, and seafood to forage. Some of the best places to forage in the area include:

- **Channel Islands National Park:** Home to various edible plants and seaweed, including wild mustard and sea lettuce.
- **Joshua Tree National Park:** This park is known for its edible cactus fruit, prickly pear, and mesquite pods.
- **San Bernardino Mountains:** This area has various edible mushrooms, including chanterelles and boletes.

- **Laguna Beach:** This area is home to edible seaweed, including kelp and sea lettuce.

Many foraging groups in Southern California provide education and resources for foragers. Some popular foraging groups in the region include:

- **Los Angeles Wild Edibles** organizes foraging walks and events throughout the Los Angeles area.
- **San Diego Mycological Society** is composed of people who love to learn about mycology, located in Lemon Grove, California. They discuss culinary, cultivation, and mushroom identification, and host forays, classes, and meetings. More information: http://sdmyco.org/
- **Orange County Mushroom Hunters:** This group focuses on finding and identifying wild mushrooms in the Orange County area.
- **Woman Forage Socal** creates a safe space for learning and personal growth through our relationship with local plants. More information https://www.womenforagesocal.com/

PART TWO
FEAST FROM THE WILD
COMMON EDIBLE PLANTS OF THE UNITED STATES

Alfalfa

Medicago sativa [MEH-DIH-KOH-GO SUH-TY-VUH]

In the 1850s, Chilean seed producers imported alfalfa to California. This perennial flowering plant belongs to the **Fabaceae** (legume) family. Common names include Lucerne, Chilean Clover, Buffalo Herb, California Clover, Purple Medic, Spanish Clover, Trefoil, Holy Hay, and Barseem.

Locate: Though widely grown as a forage crop for livestock, there are some cases where alfalfa may be found growing wild, such as in disturbed areas or along roadsides.

Identification:

GROWTH/SIZE - A perennial herb that can grow up to 3 feet tall.

BARK/STEM/ROOT - The stem is upright, smooth, and branched, with a diameter of approximately 0.2 inches. The root system is well-developed, with a taproot reaching 10-20 feet deep.

LEAF - The leaves are compound, dark green, and have smooth surfaces with serrated edges, three leaflets that are ovate to elliptical, measuring approximately 0.5-1 inch long and 0.2-0.6 inches wide.

FLOWER - The flowers are small with a distinctive clover-like shape. They are arranged in clusters on the stem, with a bright purple color. The flower clusters are generally 2-4 inches long and can produce numerous seed pods.

FRUIT/SEED/NUT - The fruit is a typically oblong pod containing several small, round seeds.

Look-a-like(s): *Sweet Clover* (*Melilotus species*) is a common roadside plant that resembles alfalfa. It has yellow or white flowers that grow in spikes and three-parted leaves. *White Clover* (*Trifolium repens*) is a common lawn plant that resembles alfalfa. It has white or pink flowers that grow in round clusters and three-parted leaves.

Caution: Alfalfa seed products may cause reactions similar to the autoimmune disease called lupus erythematous. Alfalfa might also cause some people's skin to become extra sensitive to the sun. Wear sunblock outside, especially if you are light-skinned.

Culinary Preparation: Alfalfa flowers from June to July, and the seeds ripen from July to September. Raw alfalfa leaves and sprouts have a slightly nutty and mild flavor and can be consumed raw. Healthy and flavorful, they are often used in sandwiches, smoothies, and juices. The sprouts are highly nutritious and low in calories, making them a popular choice for health-conscious consumers.

Medicinal Properties: Alfalfa is a rich source of vitamins, minerals, and antioxidants and has been used as a nutritional supplement to support overall health and well-being. Some traditional medicinal uses of alfalfa include relieving indigestion, bloating, and gas. Some modern therapeutic use studies have shown that it has prebiotic effects, which means it can help promote the growth of beneficial gut bacteria. It also has wound-healing properties and may help treat skin conditions such as psoriasis and eczema.

Fun Fact: The name "alfalfa" is derived from the Arabic word "al-fasfasah," which means "father of all foods." This name reflects the plant's reputation as a highly nutritious forage crop.

Dog Toxicity: It's generally considered safe for dogs when consumed in small amounts. Its often used as a dietary supplement and can be found in many commercial pet foods.

Allegheny Blackberry
rubus allegheniensis [ROO-BUS AL-LEH-GAY-NEE-EN-SIS]

The Allegheny Blackberry is a part of the **Rosaceae** (rose) family. They are found throughout North America. Blackberry bush growth is increased after a natural disaster such as a fire but will die back after the tree seedlings it protects start to take root and grow.

Locate: You can find blackberries at the edges of wooded areas, gardens, wastelands, along roadways, and at the edges of fields and meadows.

Identification:

GROWTH / SIZE - Blackberry bushes are easy to spot. Here are a few tidbits that should help if you aren't sure. A deciduous, native shrub that grows in a tangle of canes up to 8 ft tall and 10 feet wide.

BARK / STEM / ROOT - These stems are brown or reddish brown with stout prickles that are straight or slightly curved. The tips are green where there's new growth.

LEAF -There are usually three or ***palmately compound*** leaves with long ***petioles***. Each leaflet is up to 4" long and 3" wide; they're generally twice as long as wide. There are usually two serrated margins on an ***ovate*** leaflet. The leaves will change to Red, orange, or purple in the fall before dropping their leaves for winter.

FLOWER - Five-petaled white flowers appear in loose terminal clusters from May to June. *Racemes* of about 12 white flowers appear on the canes. No floral scent is present.

FRUIT/SEED/NUT - July is fruit season. Depending on moisture levels, *aggregate drupes* are around 3/4" long and 1/3" wide in the summer. Initially, the *drupes* are white or green, then red, then black. They're seedy and sweet when fully ripened. The fruit should come off the stem clean, revealing a solid, fleshy core.

Look-a-like(s): They can sometimes be mistaken for black raspberries, which are also edible. Several other members of the Rubus genus are similar as well.

Cautions: Take care when harvesting blackberries, and wear long sleeves; the thorns can be nasty.

Culinary Preparation: You can eat blackberries raw as you are harvesting or with a sprinkling of sugar once home for a tad of extra sweetness. They also work very well when baked into a pie or turned into jam.

Medicinal Properties: The roots are anti-hemorrhoidal, anti-rheumatic, astringent, stimulant, and tonic. An infusion can treat stomach complaints, diarrhea, piles, coughs and colds, tuberculosis, and rheumatism. The infusion has also been used by women threatened with a miscarriage. Infusions of the root can be used to soothe sore eyes. The leaves are astringent. An infusion can be used in the treatment of diarrhea. Urinary problems have been treated with an infusion of the bark. A decoction of the stems has been used as a diuretic.

Fun Fact: In the UK, some believe blackberries should not be harvested after October 11th (Old Michaelmas Day). They think that after this day, the devil will spit, step or foul the berries, making them unfit to eat. Because October is cool, humid, and often wet, a bacteria called Botryotinia can invade the berries, causing them to go rancid and causing illness.

Dog Toxicity: Not toxic to your furry friends.

Black Elderberry

Sambucus canadensis [SAM-BOO-kus kan-ah-DEN-sis]

There are two types of elderberries in the Mid-Atlantic region. The most common is the black elderberry. Still, you can find red elderberries in some parts of the state. It is a member of the **Adoxaceae** (muskroot) family. Common names are American Elder, American Elderberry, and Common Elderberry.

Locate: Elderberries like moist soil. You can find them along roadsides, trails, fences, and forests. They also grow in swamps and wasteland.

Identification:

GROWTH / SIZE - This tree is native to North America and is a woody, *deciduous* shrub or small tree that grows from 5 to 12 feet tall and 6 to 10 feet wide

BARK/STEM/ROOT - Short *lenticels* on the bark give it a warty appearance. The bark is yellowish gray to light grayish brown. A young woody branch has scattered *lenticels* that are light grayish brown. Shoots are pale green when they're young, and the *pith* is white.

LEAF - The leaves are bright green and have 5 to 11 leaflets, but most have 7. Their shape is *oval* to *lance-shaped,* measuring 2 to 6 inches long and 0.5 to 2.5 inches wide. There's a wedge-shaped base with an abruptly narrow tip. In the fall, the foliage turns yellow.

FLOWER - During June, creamy-white fragrant flowers with six petals shaped as a star appear in flat-topped or rounded clusters between 4 and 10 inches.

FRUIT /SEED/NUT - There are clusters of rounded, edible, purple-black *drupes*. The berries measure 1/4 inch across, have 3-5 seeds, and are in bulky clusters.

Look-a-like(s): *Pokeweed* (*phytolacca americana*), a plant that produces larger berries that hang in a long cylinder, and the *Devil's Walking Stick* (*Aralia spinosa*); berries are similar in appearance to elderberries, but the main stem has large thorns.

Caution: Remember that elder stems, leaves, and unripe berries are toxic and should not be consumed. Only the flowers and ripe berries are edible; the berries need to be cooked before eating. All parts of the plant contain *cyanogenic glycosides*, which are metabolized into cyanide when consumed. Cooking helps destroy the compound, making them harmless. Some mild symptoms include nausea, vomiting, and diarrhea. Elderberries can lead to coma and death if not prepared properly.

Culinary Preparation: Elderflowers can be used to make cordial or wine. The berries make a great addition to fruit pies, jams, or jellies.

Medicinal Properties: This berry is helpful for colds, touches of flu, and H1N1 "swine" flu. Additionally, it boosts your immune system and is used for HIV / AIDS. You can also use elderberry for sinus pain, back and leg pain (sciatica), nerve pain (neuropathy), and chronic fatigue syndrome (CFS).

Besides treating hay fever (allergic rhinitis) and cancer, elderberries are used as laxatives, diuretics, and sweat inducers. It can also be used to combat heart disease, high cholesterol, headaches, toothaches, and weight loss.

Fun Fact: These plants can self-pollinate, but flies are their primary pollination source.

Dog Toxicity: the leaves, stems, unripe fruit, and root are poisonous to dogs as they contain cyanide, even if only in small quantities.

Chickweed
stellaria media [STELL-AR-EE-UH MEED-EE-UH]

Chickweed grows everywhere, which is excellent news for foragers because it's almost as tasty as it is nutritious. It's also effortless to harvest. It's part of the **Caryophyllaceae** (carnation) family and has multiple names, such as starweed, Birdweed, Chickenwort, Starweed, Starwort, Winterweed, and mouse ear.

Locate: Chickweed grows almost everywhere, including backyards, parks, grasslands, fields, and wastelands.

Identification: Common chickweed is an annual in colder climates but becomes evergreen and perennial in warmer ones. It is best suited for temps between 53°F and 68°F.

GROWTH / SIZE - It grows in large patches, forming mats that can grow to 1-2 feet tall and round.

BARK/STEM/ROOT - The succulent stems are green or burgundy and often have white hairs.

LEAF - The leaves are ***oval-ovate***, broadly elliptic along their margins, hairless on top, and occasionally hairy on the bottom. The stems at the bottom of the plant have short, hairy ***petioles***, while the leaves near the tip are ***sessile***. They are more prominent at the tips of the stems, spanning up to ¾ inch in length and ½ inch across.

FLOWER - There are white, small flowers with distinctly lobed petals. In most cases, there are three stamens and three styles. The flowers don't take long to form capsules; a plant can have both flowers and capsules.

FRUIT/SEED /NUT - Seed capsules replace each flower; they're light brown, with six small teeth along their upper rim and several seeds. Mature seeds are reddish brown, slightly flattened, and orbicular-reniform; they have minute bumps on their surface.

Look-a-like(s): One toxic look-alike is the scarlet pimpernel. You can tell the difference by looking for the line of fine hairs along the stem, as the scarlet pimpernel doesn't have it. The flowers are also reddish-orange, and the plant itself has milky sap.

Caution: Nausea, upset stomach, diarrhea, and vomiting can result from too much chickweed.

Culinary Preparation: You can eat chickweed raw in salads or use it to make pestos or green smoothies. Chickweed will keep in the fridge for a few days if you wrap it in a damp paper towel and put it in a plastic bag. It also freezes reasonably well if you blend it up first.

Medicinal Properties: Soothing, cooling, hydrating, and healing, chickweed has it all for skin inflammation, wounds, boils, rashes, acne, and drawing out infections. It's applied topically as a plant poultice or infused in olive oil. Our ability to absorb nutrients improves when we eat chickweed. Combining this with the high fiber and mineral content makes chickweed a highly effective digestive support aid.

Fun Fact: Chickweed makes excellent food for poultry as well.

Dog Toxicity: Chickweed is not toxic for dogs; quite the opposite. There are several uses for chickweed when it comes to your best friend.

- **Hotspots and Skin irritation:** make a poultice using chickweed to soothe burns, hotspots, and skin irritations.
- **Tinctures:** used as an astringent to help clean and heal minor skin wounds by applying juice fresh from the stem.
- **Tea:** because it's tasty and easy for pups to digest, it can be used to soothe the occasional upset stomach.

Chicory
cichorium intybus [SIK-KOR-ee-um IN-tye-bus]

Chicory is incredibly common, and once you know what to look for, you'll probably find it everywhere. It belongs to the **Asteraceae** (daisy) family. It is known by several names, such as blue daisy, blue dandelion, blue sailors, blueweed, coffee weed, cornflower, horseweed, and wild endive.

Locate: Chicory grows readily in disturbed areas, like wastelands, meadows, fields, and roadsides.

Identification:

GROWTH /SIZE - You can spot chicory by looking for distinctive blueish-purple flowers. This biennial plant grows from two to four feet tall and one foot wide.

BARK/STEM/ROOT - It has erect green or reddish-brown stems with a fleshy taproot that exudes a milky sap when cut.

LEAF - Generally, **alternate** leaves are up to eight inches long and two inches wide, becoming smaller as they ascend the stem. These leaves are **lance-shaped** and resemble dandelion leaves at the base. The leaves gradually narrow where they are **sessile** or clasp the stem. Depending on where the leaves are on the stem, they have lobed edges, dentate edges, or they lose their **petioles** and hold the stem. In the lower leaf surface, the central vein usually has many hairs.

Flower - With numerous bright blue rays and blunt-toothed edges, these flowers have *ligulate flower heads* up to 1.5 inches long. These flowers have no stalks and grow along stems, opening up in the morning and closing up by noon unless it's cloudy, appearing from mid-summer until the first frost.

Fruit/seed/nut - Has *achene* with a brown oval shape, five ribs, and blunt ends. On the broader end, there are bristles across the top.

Look-a-like(s): Chicory plants are distinctive with their flowers and have no toxic relatives. Among wildflowers, only dandelions and daisies are easily identifiable for a beginner forager.

Caution: Chicory might have been sprayed with herbicides as it's considered a weed. Avoid harvesting chicory that's too close to busy roads.

Culinary Preparation: The leaves and flowers are bitter and can be used in salads. Use sparingly and, if need be, blanch the leaves to take away some of the bitterness. In addition, chicory roots can also be roasted, ground, or blended with coffee to make a less expensive and caffeine-free beverage.

Medicinal Properties: In the laboratory, root extracts have also been shown to be antibacterial, anti-inflammatory, and mildly sedative. In addition, they slow down and weaken the pulse, as well as lower blood sugar levels. Extracts from leaves have similar effects, though they are weaker. To treat swellings, bruised leaves were used as a poultice. A root extract can treat fevers and jaundice, as well as as a diuretic and laxative.

Fun Fact: Initially brought to the United States by the colonists as a medicinal herb, chicory was cultivated by Thomas Jefferson and others as a forage crop. As it does not dry well, horses, cattle, sheep, poultry, and rabbits were usually fed green.

Dog Toxicity: Chicory is pet safe and can benefit your pet's health.

Dandelion

taraxacum officinale [TA-RAKS-UH-KUM OH-FISS-IH-NAH-LEE]

Dandelions are one of the most common edibles and are found all over the world. They're easy to spot, which makes them a fantastic foraging option for beginners. They belong to the **Asteraceae** (daisy) family and have only one different name: Lion's tooth.

Locate: Dandelions prefer shady, cooler areas, but you'll also find them in direct sunlight. To the distaste of many homeowners, they grow on lawns. Potential habitats include parks, pastures, orchards, hayfields, meadows, and disturbed areas such as roadsides and wastelands.

Identification:

GROWTH/SIZE - You can quickly identify Dandelions by their distinctive yellow blooms. It is a fast-spreading broadleaf perennial weed that spreads by seed. The plant grows 2-6 inches tall and can get as wide as 2 feet.

BARK/STEM/ROOT - Leafless and unbranched hollow stems form deep taproots, and milky latex sap flows throughout the plant.

LEAF - A *basal rosette* is formed in an *oblanceolate* shape. Deeply toothed, backward-pointing teeth or lobes are present on rosette leaves at the base.

Flower - A bright yellow ray flower with toothed tips appears throughout the year on second-year plants. In the evening, they close their petals, single heads on their stems.

Fruit/seed/nut - Seed heads are fluffy, round, downy, and dispersed by the wind.

Look-a-like(s): *Cat's Ear* (*Hypochaeris radicata*) is the most likely to be mistaken for a dandelion, as the flower heads look very similar. Cat's Ear does not have hollow stems, and their stems are branching. They also have hairy leaves with deep notches. *Sow Thistle* (*Sonchus spp.*) also does not have hollow stems, and the leaves grow up the entire stalk with multiple flowers growing from each branch. In the thistle family, the mature plant also has prickly spines.

Caution: No plant-related, but check if they have been sprayed with a weed killer before eating.

Culinary Preparation: The entire dandelion plant is edible, but you must prepare the greens and the root differently. The greens can be eaten raw or added to salads, they have an earthy and bitter taste, and it's best to use young leaves. The leaves can also be sautéed in olive oil and garlic and seasoned. Flowers can make dandelion wine, syrups, or even baked like zucchini blossoms. Chopping and roasting the roots can be used to create tea.

Medicinal Properties: The dandelion is a commonly used herbal remedy. It is especially effective and valuable as a diuretic because it contains high potassium salts and can replace the potassium lost from the body when used. The plant is used internally to treat gall bladder and urinary disorders, gallstones, jaundice, cirrhosis, dyspepsia with constipation, edema associated with high blood pressure and heart weakness, chronic joint and skin complaints, gout, eczema, and acne. The latex contained in the plant sap can be used to remove corn, warts, and verrucae.

Fun Fact: The yellow flowers can be dried and ground into a yellow-pigmented powder and used as a dye.

Dog Toxicity: Dandelion, though not toxic, can cause constipation and gas in some dogs. Your pup can eat the whole plant if you find a fresh patch. The dandelion will boost its immune system and help improve digestion. It also aids in building strong bones and teeth.

D og Rose
rosa canina [ROH-SUH KUH-NYE-NUH]

Roses aren't just beautiful. Some roses produce fruits called rosehips. Rosehips are the bulbous area under the flower itself. They are called the fruit of the rose and come in striking colors such as red to orange, and you can even find black or yellow varieties. They are easily found in the wild and belong to the **Rosaceae** (rose) family. Other common names are Brier Hip, Dog Brier, Dog Rose Fruit, Hip Berries, Witches Brier, and Hip Rose. Several types of roses produce rosehips. Check out these varieties for your best shot at finding your prize. Dog Rose (Rosa canina), Rugosa Rose (Rosa rugosa), Prickly Wild Rose (Rosa acicularis), and Cinnamon Rose (Rosa cinnamomea).

Locate: Roses are an excellent beginner forage; they are well-known and easily spotted. Wild roses can be found in fields, scrub, and disturbed areas along roadsides, hiking trails, and woodland edges.

Identification:

GROWTH / SIZE - the plant is a shrub and grows rapidly to a height of 9 feet

BARK / STEM / ROOT - this shrub has very sharp, stout, curving thorns.

LEAF - There are 5–7 leaflets on its ***pinnate*** leaves with teeth lining the edge of the leaf blade. When bruised, the leaves smell amazing. As the weather gets colder, the leaves drop.

FLOWER - The flowers are usually pale pink but can also be deep pink or white. They bloom from June to July. Each flower has five petals and measures approximately 1.6-2.4 inches. When the *sepals* are viewed from underneath, two are whiskered (or bearded) on both sides, two are smooth, and one has a whisker (or beard) on just one side.

FRUIT/SEED/NUT - the rosehips ripen from October to December and tend to be sweeter after the first frost.

Look-a-like(s): Several wild rose species can be found while foraging. Wild strawberries, hawthorn, and crab apple are other wildflowers in the rose family. Briars, brambles, raspberries, and cloudberries are all close relatives you will likely find on your journey.

Caution: As with other thorny plants, avoid getting injured while harvesting the fruit. Below the fruit's flesh is a layer of hair around the seeds. If you eat them, they can irritate your mouth and digestive tract.

Culinary Preparation: The wild dog rose is considered the best rosehip source. Rosehips can be made into syrup as a great way to add more vitamin C to your diet. You can make jams, jellies, and pies or use them to make tea or wine.

Medicinal Properties: They're a brilliant source of vitamin C, up to 20 times more than oranges. Rosehips contain Lycopene and carotene, like carrots. Therefore, it makes sense that they would benefit the skin and eyes.

Fun Fact: Rosehips have gained plenty of notoriety in the beauty and healthcare industries for several reasons. Let's start with the beauty industry; Rosehip oil has been used for years to delay the signs of aging, though there is little scientific proof.

Dog Toxicity: You don't have to worry about your dog getting sick from roses. Their flowers, petals, and rose hips are non-toxic.

Purslane

Portulaca oleracea [POR-TEW-LAK-UH AWL-LUR-RAY-SEE-UH]

Purslane is another weed common throughout North America and Eurasia. Some people deliberately cultivate it, but once you know how to spot it, you can quickly harvest it from the wild. It is part of the Portulacaceae (purslane) family and goes by these other names: Garden Purslane, Little Hogweed, Moss Rose, Pigweed, Portulaca, Red Root, Rock Moss, Verdolaga, and Wild Portulaca.

Locate: Purslane grows in wastelands and disturbed areas, such as gravelly soil and cracks in the sidewalk.

Identification:

GROWTH/SIZE - IT's a low-growing, succulent annual plant that can grow up to 8 inches in height and 18 inches in width.

BARK/STEM /ROOT - The stem is fleshy and reddish-green, with a prostrate growth habit that produces many lateral branches. The roots are fibrous and shallow.

LEAF - The leaves are small, oval-shaped, ranging from 0.5 to 1.5 inches long. They are fleshy and succulent and range in color from green to red. The leaves grow alternately along the stem and have a smooth surface.

FLOWER - The flowers are small and cup-shaped, measuring approximately 0.5 to 0.75

inches in diameter. They are typically yellow but also pink, white, or red. The flowers bloom in the summer months and are produced in the axils of the leaves.

Fruit/seed/nut - The fruit is a small capsule that contains many tiny, black seeds. The seeds are approximately 0.05 inches in diameter and are dispersed by wind and water. The plant also reproduces by rooting at the nodes of the stem, allowing it to spread rapidly and form dense mats on the ground.

Look-a-like(s): As mentioned before, spurges are the closest toxic look-alike to Purslane. The easiest way to tell the difference is to look for fleshy, succulent leaves. Spurges have flatter leaves and exude white latex when broken.

Caution: It may interact with certain medications, digestive upset or allergic reactions.

Culinary Preparation: Immerse your collected Purslane in water to eliminate seeds and dirt. Get rid of thick stems and store them in the refrigerator. It has a mild, lemony flavor with a nice crunch. You can eat it raw in salads and sandwiches or steam it as a side dish. It also makes a delicious soup.

Medicinal Properties: It has been used for medicinal purposes for centuries in traditional Ayurveda, Chinese, and Unani cultures. Here are some traditional medicinal uses: anti-inflammatory properties due to the presence of flavonoids. It improves digestion and relieves constipation. Treats wounds, burns, and skin infections. It treats respiratory ailments such as asthma, coughs, and bronchitis. Its also used in modern medicine for its potential health benefits. Here are some of the contemporary medicinal uses of Portulaca oleracea: studies have shown that Portulaca oleracea may have anti-cancer effects, potentially due to its high antioxidant content and ability to inhibit cancer cell growth.

Fun Fact: It was a popular food among ancient Greeks and Romans, who believed it to have medicinal properties and ate it as a vegetable. The plant was also a common food source among Native Americans, who used it to make porridge or boil it as a green vegetable.

Dog Toxicity: Purslane is toxic to your pup and can cause a metabolic imbalance. Some signs of metabolic imbalance are hypersalivation, weakness, and tremors. If your dog exhibits these symptoms, it could be at risk for kidney failure.

PART THREE
NATURE'S BOUNTY
EXPLORING CALIFORNIA'S WILD FRUITS AND BERRIES

American Black Nightshade

solanum americanum [SO-LAY-NUM UH-MEH-RIH-KAY-NUM]

It is a **Solanaceae** (nightshade) family member, including tomatoes, potatoes, peppers, and eggplants. Makoi, Kakamach, Apple of Sodom, Popolo-kikania, hound's berry, and Poisonberry are familiar names.

Locate: Found in coastal areas, wetlands, pastures, woodlands, fields, roadsides, or other disturbed sites. Common among rocks, sandy beaches, trails, woods, and fields.

Identification:

GROWTH/SIZE - can grow up to 3 feet tall and 2 feet wide.

BARK/STEM/ROOT - The stem is green, cylindrical, and slightly hairy, with multiple branches. The roots are thin and fibrous.

LEAF - simple, alternate, and oval to lance-shaped, measuring about 2-4 inches long and 1-2 inches wide. They are dark green on top and lighter on the underside, with slightly serrated edges.

FLOWER - small and white, with five petals and yellow stamens. They are arranged in clusters at the end of branches and measure about 1/2 inch in diameter.

FRUIT/SEED/NUT - a small, round, green, or yellow berry that measures about 1/4 inch round. It contains many tiny, flat, yellowish seeds.

Look-a-like(s): *Black Nightshade* (*Solanum nigrum*) is edible and grows in the same areas. The critical difference is that the fruit of Black Nightshade turns black when it ripens. *Deadly Nightshade* (*Atropa belladonna*) This plant has similar-looking leaves and fruit, but the fruit of the deadly nightshade is black and shiny. Deadly nightshade can cause hallucinations, seizures, and even death if consumed.

Caution: This plant's leaves and immature green berries poison humans and animals. Poisoning symptoms include abdominal pain, vomiting, diarrhea, and possible death. The ripe berry is edible but can be toxic in large quantities.

Culinary Preparation: Flowers bloom from May to August, and berries from July to November. Blanching the leaves in boiling water for about a minute and then rinsing them in cold water will remove the bitterness. As a result, the leaves become tender and palatable. Stir-frying them with garlic and other vegetables can make a delicious side dish once blanched. Alternatively, the leaves can be boiled or dried and used as a substitute for spinach in many dishes. Add them to soups, stews, and curries for flavor and nutrition. You can eat the small fruits raw or cooked. Several types of jams, jellies, pies, tarts, and chutney can be made from them. Drying the fruits preserves them for later use by grinding and using them as a spice in cooking.

Medicinal Properties: Traditional medicinal uses include pain relief, wound healing, anti-inflammatory, respiratory disorders, and fever relief. Modern medicinal studies show it also has antimicrobial and analgesic properties that may be useful in treating conditions such as headaches and toothaches. The antioxidants may help promote overall health and well-being, and their anti-diabetic properties may help manage diabetes.

Fun Fact: Black nightshade is cultivated as a food crop on several continents, including Africa and North America. The leaves of cultivated strains are eaten after cooking.

Dog Toxicity: the whole plant is poisonous to your pup. Symptoms such as vomiting, diarrhea, drooling, abdominal pain, loss of appetite, lethargy, and disorientation can occur. They may experience seizures, respiratory distress, and even death in severe cases.

Black Currant
Ribes lacustre [RYE-BEEZ LUH-KUSS-TER]

Part of the *Grossulariaceae* (Currant) family. Common names include Black Swamp Currant, Swamp Black Gooseberry, Prickly Black Gooseberry, Black Gooseberry, Black Bristly Currant, Spiny Swamp Gooseberry, and Swamp Goose Currant.

It is found in moist woods, swamps, streambanks, drier forest slopes, and subalpine ridges.

Identification:

GROWTH/SIZE - a deciduous shrub that can grow 6 feet tall and 6 feet wide.

BARK/STEM/ROOT - The bark of the stem is dark brown and covered with shallow fissures, while the roots are fibrous and spread out shallowly.

LEAF - simple, alternate, and lobed, 1-3 inches long and 1-2 inches wide. The leaf margins are serrated, and the leaf surface is smooth, glossy, and dark green.

FLOWER - small and inconspicuous, 1/8 to 1/4 inch long. They are bell-shaped, with five petals that are pink to red. The flowers bloom in late spring to early summer.

FRUIT/SEED/NUT - small, black berries about a 1/4 inch round. They are covered in fine hair and have a sweet, tart flavor. The seeds are small measuring less than 1/8 inch long.

Look-a-like(s): *Wild gooseberry* (*Ribes hirtellum*) has lobed leaves and produces small, edible berries. The berries are typically green or yellow rather than black. *Golden currant* (*Ribes aureum*) has a similar growth habit with lobed leaves and small, bell-shaped flowers. However, the flowers are yellow rather than pink or red, and the berries are larger and yellowish-green.

Caution: The leaves, stems, and seeds contain small amounts of hydrocyanic acid, which can be toxic in large quantities. In general, the levels of this compound are not high enough to pose a threat, so seeds are usually consumed with fruit without a problem.

Culinary Preparation: Black currants can be eaten fresh from the bush or added to salads, smoothies, or fruit bowls. They have a sweet, tart flavor that pairs well with other fruits and vegetables. They are a popular ingredient in jams, jellies, and preserves and can be made into syrup or sauce for pancakes or ice cream. They can be added to all types of baked goods for a burst of flavor or turned into a refreshing summertime drink when mixed with water, sugar, and lemon.

Medicinal Properties: It's a rich source of antioxidants, has anti-inflammatory properties and contains other immune-supporting compounds, such as anthocyanins, to help protect against infections and improve vision in people with certain eye conditions, such as glaucoma. It also contains fiber and may help support digestive health and prevent constipation.

Fun Fact: This prickly shrub was thought to have protective qualities to ward off evil and was used to discourage snakes. The roots were used to make rope and reef nets. The sharp thorns have been used as probes for boils, removing splinters, and tattooing.

Dog Toxicity: generally considered safe for dogs; however, the leaves and stems of black currant contain small amounts of hydrocyanic acid, which can be toxic in large quantities.

Blackthorn
Prunus spinosa [PROO-nus spy-NO-suh]

In Irish folklore, it was believed that "the little people" lived in blackthorn bushes. It's a species of flowering plant in the **Rosaceae** (rose) family. It is popularly known as the Mother of the wood, wishing thorn, wild plum, winter picks, Sloe-Bush, stickleback, and Sloe of Europe.

Locate: Moist draws, thickets, hillsides, roadsides, and railroads.

Identification:

GROWTH/SIZE - a deciduous shrub or small tree that typically grows 10 to 20 feet tall and has a spread of 6 to 10 feet.

BARK/STEM/ROOT - The bark of the mature plants is dark gray, rough, and fissured, while the stems are thorny and spiny, with thorns up to 1 inch long. The roots are shallow and fibrous, spreading widely.

LEAF - ovate to elliptical, dark green on the upper surface and paler on the underside, with finely serrated margins.

FLOWER - produced in early spring before the leaves emerge. They are white, small, and star-shaped, measuring around 0.6 inches in diameter. The petals are arranged in clusters of 2-5 and have a strong, sweet fragrance.

FRUIT/SEED/NUT - small, oval-shaped drupes, commonly known as sloes. They are bluish-black and measure around 0.4 to 0.6 inches round. The seeds are large and hard, measuring around 0.2 to 0.3 inches in length.

Look-a-like(s): *Hawthorn* (*Crataegus spp.*) produces white or pink flowers in spring, followed by red or black berries in the fall. The leaves are similar but often have deeper-lobed edges. The *Cherry Plum* (*Prunus cerasifera*) is a small tree or shrub that produces pink or white blossoms in spring, followed by small plum-like fruit in summer. There are similar leaves, but the bark lacks thorns and is smooth.

Caution: Blackthorn has long, sharp thorns that can cause injury. When handling, it is essential to wear gloves and protective clothing to avoid getting scratched.

Culinary Preparation: The berries taste bitter though they are better if harvested after the 2nd frost. The fruit tastes sour and is often used to make jams, jellies, and sloe gin.

Medicinal Properties: Blackthorn is known to have astringent properties, which can help to tone and strengthen the digestive system. It's rich in vitamin C, vital for immune system function. It is also a good source of antioxidants, which can help to protect the body against inflammation. It's been used topically to treat various skin conditions, including eczema, psoriasis, and acne, and is sometimes used to support women's health, particularly during menopause. It is believed to help regulate hormonal imbalances and ease hot flashes and other menopausal symptoms.

Fun Fact: The branches are traditionally used as walking sticks or clubs, called shille-laghs in Ireland.

Dog Toxicity: Dogs shouldn't be fed Sloeberries. Most dogs dislike Sloeberries because of their tart flavor. Although sloe berries are not toxic for dogs, excessive consumption may lead to diarrhea and other digestive problems.

C rowberry
Empetrum nigrum [EM-PEE-TRUM NY-GRUM]

The Scottish Highlands Clan Maclean's badge is believed to be a Black Crowberry; cuttings of it would be raised on standards to denote clan identity and allegiance. It is a flowering plant species in the **Ericaceae** (heather) family. Common names are Crowberry, Black crowberry, Mossberry, and curlewberry.

Locate: It can be found on cliffs, balds, ledges, mountain summits and plateaus, ridges or ledges, sandplains, and barrens.

Identification:

GROWTH/SIZE - a small, evergreen shrub that typically grows between 2 and 24 inches tall and spreads to form a low mat.

BARK/STEM/ROOT - The stems are slender, woody, and often creeping, with a diameter of 0.1-0.2 inches. The bark is smooth and grayish-brown. The roots are fibrous and shallow, enabling the plant to grow in poor soils and harsh climates.

LEAF - simple, alternate, and evergreen. They are lanceolate or oblong, measuring 0.2-0.6 inches long and 0.1-0.2 inches wide. The leaves are dark green, glossy, and leathery, with a revolute margin that helps to reduce water loss and protect the plant from wind and cold.

FLOWER - produces small, inconspicuous flowers that are borne in the axils of the leaves. The flowers are bell-shaped and are usually reddish-purple or greenish-yellow.

FRUIT/SEED/NUT - The berry is a small, black drupe with a slightly sweet and tart flavor and can hang on the plant all winter.

Look-a-like(s): *Bog Bilberry* (*Vaccinium uliginosum*) is a low-growing, deciduous shrub. Its leaves are oval or elliptical. Its flowers are pink or white, bell-shaped, and appear in early summer. Its fruits are blue-black, berry-like drupes that are edible. *Bearberry* (*Arctostaphylos uva-ursi*) is a spreading evergreen shrub. Its leaves are oval and leathery. Its pink or white flowers are urn-shaped and appear in late spring. Its fruits are bright red, berry-like drupes that are edible.

Caution: The berries contain oxalic acid, which can be toxic in large amounts. Consuming large quantities may cause digestive discomforts, such as nausea, vomiting, or diarrhea.

Culinary Preparation: The berries are harvested between August and September when they are fully ripe. They can be dried or used to make tea with antioxidants. Cooked into a thick, flavorful jam or jelly or added to various desserts, such as pies, tarts, muffins, and cakes. They can be made into syrup and used as a drink sweetener or on pancakes, waffles, or ice cream. Or they can be used fresh or frozen and added to the batter or filling.

Medicinal Properties: It has been used as a diuretic, especially for children with fevers. Diarrhea has been treated with a decoction or infusion of the stems, or cooked berries, and the roots have been used as an eyewash to remove growths.

Fun Fact: Crowberry can survive more than 20 years in the wild. In Labrador, people call the fruits of crowberry plants "blackberry." They generally burn the leaves and stems of the plant for smoking fish, especially salmon, Arctic char, and sea trout.

Dog Toxicity: Not toxic to your pups.

Cascade Bilberry

Vaccinium deliciosum [VUH-SIN-EE-UM DEH-LIH-SOH-SUM]

The bilberry has been used for over 1000 years in traditional European medicine. It's a member of the **Ericaceae** (heather) family, and other familiar names are Cascade huckleberry or blue huckleberry.

Locate: It can be found in various habitats, including mountain slopes, forests, and meadows. It's often found growing with other plants, such as Douglas fir, western hemlock, and red alder.

Identification:

GROWTH/SIZE - A shrub native to California that can grow up to 5-6 feet tall and wide.

BARK/STEM/ROOT - The bark is thin and smooth, and the stems are woody, with new growth appearing green and turning reddish-brown with age. The roots are fibrous and shallow, with no taproot.

LEAF - The leaves are oval-shaped, measuring 2 inches long and an inch wide. They are green and glossy on the upper surface and pale on the underside. The edges of the leaves are smooth, and the tips are pointed.

FLOWER - The flowers are bell-shaped, white, or pinkish, measuring around a 1/2 inch long. They bloom from late spring to early summer.

Fruit/seed/nut - the berry is round or flattened, measuring around 1/2 inch in diameter. It's blue-black and has a sweet and tangy flavor. The seeds are small and numerous.

Look-a-like(s): *Black huckleberry* (*Vaccinium membranaceum*) is similar in appearance, with small oval leaves and clusters of dark berries. The berries are usually black or dark purple. *Salal* (*Gaultheria shallon*) is a low-growing shrub with similar shiny, oval leaves. However, the leaves are thicker and more leathery. It also produces edible purple-black berries.

Caution: Caution is advised if you have diabetes, alcohol dependence, or liver disease.

Culinary Preparation: As with every other berry we have covered, the berries can be eaten fresh, used in baking, to make jams, jellies, preserves, and sauces, or mixed with juices, smoothies, and cocktails.

Medicinal Properties: Some of the traditional uses include as a digestive aid, anti-inflammatory, and treatment for urinary tract infections and respiratory ailments such as coughs, bronchitis, and asthma, and it is a rich source of antioxidants. Some preliminary modern studies have suggested an antimicrobial effect that may be effective against certain bacteria and viruses. Anti-diabetic effects may help regulate blood sugar levels, improve insulin sensitivity, and increase cognitive function.

Fun Fact: It was traditionally used as a dye in Britain for food and clothes because it stains hands, teeth, and tongue deep blue or purple when eaten. The blue or black dye obtained from the fruit can be used as ink. The leaves produce a green dye used for coloring fabrics.

Pet Toxicity: They are generally considered safe for pets when consumed in small amounts. However, consuming large quantities of blue huckleberry may cause gastrointestinal upset, such as vomiting or diarrhea.

Goji Berry

Lycium barbarum [LYE-SEE-UM BAA-BUH-RUM]

Goji Berries have been used in traditional Chinese medicine for over 2000 years, with early records tracing back to the Tang Dynasty. A flowering plant in the **Solanaceae** (nightshade) family. Chinese wolfberry, barbary matrimony vine, red medlar, or matrimony vine are familiar names.

Locate: They can grow in sunny, well-drained areas, such as hillsides and mountainsides, hedges, walls, and waste ground.

Identification:

GROWTH/SIZE - deciduous shrub grows up to 10 feet tall and 10 feet wide.

BARK/STEM/ROOT - Its bark is grey-brown, and its stems are woody and thorny. The root system is extensive, with deep roots reaching 10 feet long.

LEAF - The leaves are lance-shaped and measure up to 3 inches long. They are arranged alternately on the stem and are bright green.

FLOWER - The flowers are trumpet-shaped and measure up to 1 inch long. They are purple-red in color and bloom in the summer.

FRUIT/SEED/NUT - The fruit is a small, bright red berry that is oval and measures up to 1 inch long. The seeds are small, numerous, and embedded in the fruit's flesh.

Look-a-like(s): *Bittersweet nightshade* (*Solanum dulcamara*) has similar-looking leaves and berries, but the berries are poisonous and should not be eaten. *Ground cherry* (*Physalis pruinosa*) is a fruit enclosed in a papery husk. The fruit is edible and is often used in jams and desserts.

Caution: Goji berries may cause allergic reactions in some people. Itching, swelling, and difficulty breathing can be symptoms of an allergic reaction. Certain medications, such as blood thinners and diabetes medications, may interact with goji berries.

Culinary Preparation: It is important to note that they are tough to chew. Soaking them in water for a few minutes to soften them will make them easier to eat. Goji berries can be eaten raw as a snack, added to trail mix, or sprinkled on top of yogurt, oatmeal, or a salad. They can be steeped in hot water to make a tea rich in antioxidants and nutrients. They can also be added to baked goods such as muffins, bread, and cookies or put in granola bars or energy bites and added to smoothies to boost nutrients and flavor.

Medicinal Properties: Goji berries are rich in antioxidants, which can help boost the immune system. They contain high levels of **zeaxanthin** and **lutein**, essential eye health nutrients. They can help protect against age-related macular degeneration and other eye conditions. They may help regulate blood sugar levels, improve insulin sensitivity, and help protect the liver from damage caused by toxins and other harmful substances.

Fun Fact: Goji berries were initially grown in Tibet, look like a tomato, and taste like a cherry. They have many of the same antioxidant properties as tomatoes, with high levels of vitamins C, B, and E and calcium.

Pet Toxicity: Moderate amounts of goji berries are safe for dogs. They can improve the health of muscles, nerves, bones, and enzymes. Goji berries may provide a boost in immunity.

Marsh berry

Vaccinium oxycoccus [VUH-SIN-ee-um OKS-ee-KOK-us]

Cranberry sauce is a traditional accompaniment to turkey at Thanksgiving and Christmas dinners in the United States. It is known as small cranberry, bog cranberry, and swamp cranberry and is a flowering plant in the **Ericaceae** (heather) family.

Locate: It can be harvested in wetland habitats such as bogs, marshes, and wet meadows.

Identification:

GROWTH/SIZE - a small evergreen shrub that grows up to 6 inches tall and spreads up to 2 feet wide.

BARK/STEM/ROOT - Its bark is brownish-gray, and the stem is woody, thin, and flexible, measuring up to 4 inches long. The roots are shallow and fibrous, spreading horizontally to the soil's surface.

LEAF - The leaves are simple, alternate, and elliptical. They are dark green on the upper surface and pale green on the lower surface. The margins are slightly rolled under.

FLOWER - The flowers are small, pinkish-white, and bell-shaped. They grow in clusters of 2-5 and bloom from May to June.

FRUIT/SEED/NUT - The fruit is a round, red berry with four locules and contains many tiny seeds.

Look-a-like(s): *Lingonberry* (*Vaccinium vitis-idaea*) is a closely related species of cranberry and looks very similar. *Wintergreen* (*Gaultheria procumbens*) is a small evergreen plant that grows in similar habitats as small cranberry. It has glossy green leaves that have a distinct minty smell when crushed. The fruits are red, but they are not edible.

Caution: Some people may be allergic to small cranberry and experience hives, itching, or difficulty breathing symptoms. It can interact with prescription medication, so consult with your healthcare provider.

Culinary Preparation: Marsh berries are often used to make a sauce, juice, jam, and relish. They can also be used in baking to make treats like muffins or bread. They can also replace the traditional store-bought cranberries around the holidays.

Medicinal Properties: Marsh berry is known for its ability to prevent and treat urinary tract infections (UTIs), promote digestion, relieve digestive problems such as diarrhea, bloating, and gas, and help protect the heart and blood vessels from oxidative damage. They also have anti-inflammatory properties, which may help reduce inflammation and alleviate pain and discomfort.

Fun Fact: Some Iñupiat cook the cranberry with fish eggs and blubber. Europeans named the fruit "crane berry" because they thought the blossom looked like the head of a sandhill crane.

Dog Toxicity: Both fresh and dried cranberries are safe to feed to dogs in small quantities. Whether your dog will like this tart treat is another question. Either way, moderation is essential when feeding cranberries to dogs, as with any treat, as too many can lead to an upset stomach.

Northern Dewberry

Rubus flagellaris [ROO-bus flaj-uh-LAIR-iss]

Dewberry is native to North America and has been used for erosion control and wildlife habitat restoration. The plant is valued for stabilizing soil, preventing erosion, and providing food and cover for various wildlife species. It's a perennial shrub in the **Rosaceae** (rose) family. Familiar names include Northern dewberry, American dewberry, Running blackberry, and Trailing blackberry.

Locate: It is typically found growing in open woods, meadows, and along forest edges and is particularly common in areas with moist, well-drained soils.

Identification:

GROWTH/SIZE - a deciduous shrub that grows up to 3 feet tall and 6 feet wide.

BARK/STEM/ROOT - The stems are thorny and green when young turning reddish brown as they mature. They are slender and flexible. The roots are fibrous and shallow, spreading horizontally beneath the soil's surface.

LEAF - The leaves are palmately compound, with three to five leaflets that are oval or oblong in shape and measure 1 to 3 inches long and 1/2 to 1 inch wide. The leaflets are dark green and shiny on top and pale and fuzzy underneath. They are arranged alternately along the stem.

FLOWER - The flowers are white or pink, with five petals that measure 1/2 to 3/4 inches across. They appear in early summer, from May to June, and are borne singly or in small clusters on the ends of the branches.

FRUIT/SEED/NUT - The fruit is a juicy, edible berry that is dark red to black and measures 1/2 to 3/4 inches across. The berry comprises many small, fleshy drupelets containing a single, hard seed. The fruit ripens in mid-summer, from July to August, and is sweet and flavorful.

Look-a-like(s): *Allegheny blackberry* (*Rubus allegheniensis*), *Pennsylvania blackberry* (*Rubus pensilvanicus*), and *Black raspberry* (*Rubus occidentalis*) are all edible and can be confused with dewberry. As a part of the Rubus family, all four plants have telltale thorns.

Caution: The flowers, with their fragrant nectar, attract many native bees. They also provide nesting materials and structures for the native bees. It frequently shares a habitat with poison ivy.

Culinary Preparation: Northern dewberries can be eaten fresh or used in various recipes, such as jams, jellies, pies, and syrups. Harvest the berries when they are ripe, typically in mid-summer. Look for berries that are fully colored and plump, with a sweet aroma. Northern dewberries can also make delicious syrup or be frozen for later use. The dried leaves make a fantastic tea.

Medicinal Properties: The root is an astringent, stimulant, and tonic. The leaves and roots were used to make a tea that was taken internally to reduce inflammation and swelling and assist with digestion and stomach cramps. Creating a poultice from the leaves and roots helps promote healing and helps prevent infection in superficial wounds and sores. It was also used to help increase urine production and promote the elimination of toxins from the body.

Fun Fact: The fruit is an essential summer food source to many upland gamebirds, songbirds, and mammals, while rabbits and deer browse on the leaves and stems.

Dog Toxicity: These berries are not toxic to your pet.

W estern Serviceberry

amelanchier alnifolia [UH-MUH-LAN-CHEE-ER AL-NI-FOH-LEE-UH]

Western Serviceberry is an excellent choice for native gardens in Northern California and throughout the Sierras. Great for attracting birds and other small animals. It's a member of the **Rosaceae** (Rose) family. Common names are the Saskatoon berry, Pacific serviceberry, western shadbush, or western juneberry.

Locate: It can be found in thickets, woodland edges, streambanks, and moist, well-drained soils.

Identification:

GROWTH/SIZE - a deciduous shrub that typically grows to a height of 6-15 feet and a spread of 4-10 feet.

BARK/STEM/ROOT - The bark is smooth and gray, and the stems are slender and branching. The root system is fibrous and shallow, spreading out to anchor the shrub in the ground.

LEAF - The leaves are oval-shaped and serrated, measuring 1-2 inches long. They are green, with a glossy surface and a slightly fuzzy underside.

FLOWER - The flowers are white and star-shaped, with five petals and a yellow center. They typically measure around 1 inch in diameter and bloom in late spring to early summer.

FRUIT/SEED/NUT - The fruit is a small, dark purple berry that is sweet and edible. The berries typically measure around 1/2 inch in diameter.

Look-a-like(s): *Blueberry* (*Vaccinium sp.*) Blueberries are deciduous shrubs that produce white flowers and berries, but the leaves are generally narrower and lance-shaped. *Snowberry* (*Symphoricarpos sp.*) This plant is a deciduous shrub with white or pink flowers and small, white berries. The leaves are similar in shape, but the flowers and berries are more petite. Both of these are edible, so there is nothing to worry about.

Caution: none known

Culinary Preparation: Because of its sweet and slightly nutty flavor, it's a versatile ingredient. A delicious jam spread for toast or pastries can be made or add a splash of color and flavor to muffins, cakes, and pies. They can also be used to flavor tea or lemonade, make smoothies, or add to yogurt.

Medicinal Properties: Traditionally, the berries were used to help with digestive problems, including diarrhea, constipation, and stomach aches. The leaves were used to make a tea or infusion that was thought to help with respiratory issues, such as coughs, sore throats, and congestion. The roots and bark were used to make a poultice that could be applied topically to relieve pain and inflammation. According to some modern studies, antioxidants found in the berries may help protect cells from damage. It has anti-inflammatory properties that help treat inflammation-related diseases such as arthritis. Some studies have suggested that the berries might have anti-cancer properties and potential benefits for heart health.

Fun Fact: Its wood is hard, strong, fine-grained, and used for tool handles, canes, canoe crossbars, tipi stakes, tipi closure pins, and small implements. The berries can be made into a purple dye for fabrics.

Dog Toxicity: The berries are generally considered safe for pets to eat in small amounts. While the berries are usually safe, other parts of the plant, such as the leaves and bark, contain toxic compounds that can harm pets if ingested.

PART FOUR
EDIBLE WEEDS
COMMONLY FOUND WILD HERBS AND GRASSES IN CALIFORNIA

Beargrass
Xerophyllum tenax [ZEH-ROH-FILL-UM TEN-ACKS]

Lewis and Clark expedition members initially called this plant Beargrass because they saw grizzly bears using the leaves in their dens and eating the young fleshy stems. It belongs to the **Melanthiaceae** (bunchflower) family. Several familiar names refer to it, including soap grass, quip-quip, Western Turkeybeard, bear lily, pine lily, elkgrass, squawgrass, and Indian basket grass.

Location: A native of Northern California, it can be found on the Olympic Peninsula, in the Cascades, in the northern Sierra Nevadas, and the Rockies. It can be found on dry, sunny hillsides, open woods, and clearings.

Identification:

GROWTH/SIZE: a slow-growing, herbaceous perennial forming clumps of narrow leaves up to 3 feet tall.

BARK/STEM: a tough, solid, unbranched, fibrous stem. The stem can be green to yellow-green and is covered in fine, silky hairs.

LEAF: The narrow and blade-like leaves grow in a basal rosette. They are stiff with a pale green color and are covered in fine, silky hairs.

FLOWER: produces a significant, showy spike of white, bell-shaped flowers up to 10 inches long. The flowers are fragrant and bloom in late spring and early summer.

Nᴜᴛ/Sᴇᴇᴅ: Tiny, black, berry-like seeds are attached to the stem.

Look-alike Plants: *Yucca* (*Yucca filamentosa*), but its flowers can distinguish it.

Cautions: Beargrass contains small amounts of the toxin lycorine, which can cause vomiting and diarrhea if consumed in large quantities.

Culinary Preparation: Beargrass can be harvested for its leaves, stem, and flowers. Because it is slow growing, it is essential to harvest it sustainably. Beargrass roots have a bitter taste. The bitterness of the roots can be dissipated by boiling them in water or roasting them thoroughly. The seed pods are also good once roasted as long as it's before they open.

Medicinal Uses: Beargrass has been used medicinally by Native American tribes for various purposes, including as a treatment for skin irritations and wounds and as a medicinal tea. There is a styptic element in the roots. Poultices made from chewed roots have been applied to wounds. The root's decoction was applied to bleeding wounds, sprains, and broken limbs. A lather is made with the washed roots used to soothe sore eyes.

Fun Fact: Beargrass has an important cultural significance to Native American tribes in the Pacific Northwest, who use it to make baskets, ropes, and other woven items.

In its native regions, it plays a vital role in fire ecology. It has rhizomes that survive fires that purge the ground surface of dead and dying plants. Periodic burns will often increase the plant's growth, and it will usually sprout first in areas that have been scorched.

Dog Toxicity: This type of grass is too harsh for dogs to digest, so it will make them vomit. More severe reactions could include swelling of the mouth and throat, diarrhea, and muscle convulsions.

Bladderpod Spiderflower
Peritoma arborea [PE-RIH-TOH-MUH AR-BOR-EE-UH]

A perennial shrub or bush belonging to the **Cleomaceae** (Spider Flower) family. It's fire-retardant and drought-tolerant, making it a perfect choice for your garden. This plant attracts hummingbirds, hawk moths, quail, and other wild birds. Harlequin beetles, members of the stink bug family, are especially attracted to bladderpod leaves and pods. This plant has several common names, including bladderpod, California Cleome, and burro-fat.

Location: It is native to California and the Baja California Peninsula. It's commonly found along roadsides, desert washes, and flat areas in the western Mojave Desert and from the Colorado Desert to Baja California Peninsula.

Identification:

GROWTH/SIZE: An annual plant growing up to 3 feet tall.

BARK/STEM/ROOT: The stem is thin, upright, and covered in fine hairs.

LEAF: Its silvery-gray leaves have three equal leaflets, each a long, pointed oval 1 to 4 cm wide.

FLOWER: There are abundant clusters of yellow flowers at the ends of the branches. A flower usually has four petals and six whiskery stamens that protrude with curling

tips holding anthers. Long, protruding styles bear the developing fruit at their tips in
the middle.

Fruit / seed / nut: Seedpods of this plant measure up to 2 inches long. They are
swollen, drooping, and pointed at the tips. They are about the same color as the leaves
but become more tanned and sometimes transparent as they age. The seeds inside the
pod can be either white or black.

Look-a-like(s): *Spiderwort* (*Tradescantia spp.*) has similar-looking flowers, often blue,
pink, or purple. The leaves are broader and more grass-like. *Cleome* (*Cleome hassle-
riana*) has similar-looking flowers and leaves, but the leaves are more deeply lobed,
and the flowers are typically larger and showier.

Cautions: *Carolina horse nettle* (*Solanum carolinense*) has similar-looking leaves, but the
flowers are white or purple and appear more star-shaped. It's toxic and should not be
consumed. It can cause skin irritation in some people. It is also a pollen source for
bees, so be wary that you could get stung if you are not paying attention.

Culinary Preparation: The flowers and seeds of the bladderpod are edible. The
flowers and young seed pods are best enjoyed in the spring and summer. You can
make wild capers if you harvest the unopened flower buds and pickle them. The pods
are filled with seeds, which fall out like peas.

Medicinal Uses: Has been used by Native American tribes as a treatment for respiratory and digestive problems.

Fun Fact: The seedpods, when dry, resemble a paper lantern that rattles.

Dog Toxicity: Not considered toxic to dogs, but it is not recommended for them to
consume it as it can cause digestive upset.

B ride's Bonnet

Clintonia uniflora [KLIN-TOH-NEE-UH YOO-NEE-FLOR-UH]

A member of the **Liliaceae** (lily) family, other common names include queen's cup, Wolf Berry Blue Bead Lily, Clintonia, Clinton's Lily, Corn Lily, Snakeberry, Dogberry, and Cow Tongue. One characteristic distinguishing this species from others in the genus Clintonia is its specific epithet, uniflora. That's why it is also known as the single-flowered clintonia.

Location: Bride's Bonnet is native to California. Typically, it lives in a cool, moist coniferous forest composed of western red cedar, western hemlock, grand fir, subalpine fir, and Pacific silver fir.

Identification:

GROWTH / SIZE: a herbaceous perennial that grows up to 1-2 feet tall.

BARK / STEM: The stem is thin, wiry, and green, often partially or entirely hidden by the brightly colored bracts of the flowers.

LEAF: The leaves are narrow and lance-shaped, typically arranged alternately on the stem.

FLOWER: The flowers are brightly colored and arranged in spikes. They are typically red, orange, or yellow and are surrounded by bracts that are also brightly colored.

FRUIT / SEED / NUT: The plant produces tiny seeds enclosed in seed capsules.

Look-a-like(s): *Meadow Buttercup* (*Ranunculus acris*) is toxic to humans and animals. It contains the toxin protoanemonin, which can cause severe irritation and blister to the skin and mucous membranes. Ingesting parts of the plant can cause digestive issues such as nausea, vomiting, and diarrhea.

Cautions: Never consume any other parts of this plant besides the young leaves. The berries contain a toxin that is harmful to humans.

Culinary Preparation: Plants flower from late May to July, and the fruit ripens from late July to September. You can eat raw or cooked young leaves, though they are not palatable. Harvest in the spring before the leaves have unfurled. Potherbs can be made from older leaves.

Medicinal Properties: It's been used by Native American tribes for medicinal purposes, including as a treatment for skin and respiratory problems.

Fun Fact: Bride's Bonnet is a popular food source for many species of pollinators, including bees and butterflies.

Pet Toxicity: Bride's Bonnet is toxic to dogs and can cause digestive upset and other symptoms if ingested. It is essential to keep pets away from this plant.

Buffalo Gourd
cucurbita foetidissima [KYOO-KUR-BEE-TUH FEE-TUH-DIS-UH-MUH]

A member of the **Cucurbitaceae** (cucumber) family, It has numerous common names, including calabazilla, Chillicothe, coyote gourd, fetid gourd, fetid wild pumpkin, Missouri gourd, prairie gourd, stinking gourd, wild gourd, and wild pumpkin. In Latin, foetidissima means ill-smelling. It contains high amounts of protein and carbohydrates and yields abundant oil. The carbohydrates formed in the tap root have led to the idea of growing the plant for biofuel.

Location: Desert scrub, interior chaparral, semidesert grasslands, and pinyon-juniper woodlands are some of the disturbed habitats where they can be found.

Identification:

GROWTH / SIZE: Buffalo gourds can grow up to 10-12 feet long and have a 6-8 inches diameter.

BARK / STEM / ROOT: When the gourd is young, its stem is thick and woody, and its bark is smooth and green, but it turns brown and rough as it ages. The plant's tap root functions as a storage and overwintering structure.

LEAF: The leaves are large and heart-shaped, measuring 12-18 inches long.

FLOWER: The flowers are large and trumpet-shaped, measuring 4-5 inches in diameter. They are usually yellow or orange. The flowers bloom from July to September.

FRUIT / SEED / NUT: From August to October, it produces a round, hard, inedible nut that measures about 1-2 inches in diameter.

Look-a-like(s): When young, they resemble small watermelons but mature into yellow fruits.

Cautions: Children are most vulnerable because of their curiosity and small size. Toxin sensitivity varies by age, weight, physical condition, and individual susceptibility.

Culinary Preparation: The fruit can be cooked like squash when very young. As the fruit matures, it becomes bitter and unpalatable to humans. Oil-rich seeds with a nutty flavor can be roasted or boiled. You can grind them into powder and use them to thicken soups or mix them with cereal flour to make cakes and biscuits. The root is a healthy source of starch used for sweetening, stabilizing, or making puddings, such as tapioca.

Medicinal Properties: Native North American tribes used buffalo gourd medicinally, particularly for skin problems. Traditionally, mashed plant poultices have been used for treating skin sores, ulcers, and other ailments. To induce vomiting, boil peeled roots and make tea. To reduce swelling, mix powdered seeds and flowers with saliva. As a laxative, dried root is ground to a powder, mixed with cold water, and drunk.

Fun Fact: When fruit is cut into pieces and simmered in water, soap can be made to remove stains. After drying, the fruit's skin is tough, thick, and hard to break. It can be used whole as a rattle or carved into ladles, spoons, etc.

Dog Toxicity: Generally, these plants are not harmful to your dog; however, the leaves do not smell appealing, so they are more likely to roll in them instead of eating them. Your curious pup may use the melon as a toy.

California Poppy

Eschscholzia californica [ESS-SHOAL-ZEE-A KAL-IH-FOR-NI-KA]

Sarah Plummer Lemmon first advocated for the golden poppy to be adopted as the state flower of California in the 1890s. She later wrote the California Legislature's bill that was signed into law by Governor George Pardee the following year. The flowering plant belongs to the **Papaveraceae** (poppy) family. They are also known as golden poppy, California sunshine, or cup of gold.

Location: California poppy is native to California and can grow wild in grasslands, prairies, and roadsides. Northern Los Angeles County is home to the Antelope Valley California Poppy Reserve. The 1,745 acres of the reserve are covered in orange flowers during the peak of the blooming season.

Identification:

GROWTH / SIZE: California poppy is an annual or biennial herb that grows up to 60 cm tall.

BARK / STEM / ROOT: The stem is thin and delicate and covered in fine hairs.

LEAF: The leaves are silvery blue and are 3/4 to 4 inches long.

FLOWER: The most common color is bright orange, but it ranges from creamy yellow to bright orange. A 3-inch diameter, cup-shaped flower with four silky petals closes at night and in rainy or cloudy weather.

Fruit/seed/nut: Black poppy seed capsules are formed inside the blooming petals. When the capsules split open, thousands of seeds are released.

Look-a-like(s): *Mexican gold poppy* (*Eschscholzia mexicana*) has smaller flowers and is often more orange. The leaves are also more finely divided. *Arizona poppy* (*Kallstroemia grandiflora*) has similar bright yellow-orange flowers with more pointed petals. The leaves are small and divided, and the plant grows low to the ground. *Fiddleneck* (*Amsinckia spp.*) has similar bright orange-yellow flowers with a more tubular shape. The leaves are narrow and pointed, and the plant has a rough, hairy texture.

Cautions: California poppy is considered safe for human consumption in moderate amounts but can cause drowsiness or lethargy if consumed in large quantities.

Culinary Preparation: The leaves of California poppy can be used as a garnish or in salads, while the seeds can be roasted and used as a seasoning.

Medicinal Properties: Numerous medicinal properties are associated with the California poppy, making it a highly prized herb in herbalism. The herb is a sedative, relieves insomnia and nervous agitation, and promotes relaxation. In addition, it helps treat both acute and chronic liver and bladder diseases. Additionally, the California poppy is one of the best natural treatments for bed-wetting problems in children. A tea made from the chopped plant is used to treat headaches, toothaches, and insomnia.

Fun Fact: California poppy is the state flower of California and is used as a symbol of the state's natural beauty and resources. The pollen is used to make cosmetics, and flowers are used for hairdressing and hair dyeing.

Dog Toxicity: California poppy is generally considered safe for dogs, but excessive consumption can cause digestive upset or drowsiness. As with any plant, it is best to keep dogs away from this plant until you are sure they will not be harmed.

Coastal Tarweed
Madia sativa [MA-dee-uh suh-TEE-vuh]

Chilean tarweed or coastal tarweed is a species of flowering plant in the **Asteraceae** (aster) family.

Location: It grows wild in California coastal regions, in areas with well-drained soil.

Identification:

GROWTH / SIZE: An annual or biennial plant growing up to 3 feet tall.

BARK / STEM / ROOT: The stems are hairless, slender, and green to reddish-brown.

LEAF: The leaves are hairy and alternately arranged. They are lance-shaped, densely covered with sticky resin glands, and have a strong scent.

FLOWERS: The plant has either male or female flowers, but both sexes can be found on the same plant. Insects pollinate it. Generally, the inflorescence consists of clusters of flower heads lined with bristly, glandular phyllaries. Approximately eight yellowish ray florets a few millimeters long around the center of several disc florets tipped with dark anthers on each head.

FRUIT / SEED / NUT: The fruit has no pappus, which is a flat, hairless achene. The seeds ripen in late summer, usually in August in California. After gathering, seeds can be stored in a cool, dry place for at least a year and maintain viability.

Look-a-like(s): *Coyote Brush* (*Baccharis pilularis*) is a small, woody shrub commonly found along the California coast. Coyote brush has small, white, or pale pink flowers that bloom in late summer and fall. The leaves are small, narrow, and green; the plant is often covered in fine hairs. *California Sagebrush* (*Artemisia californica*) has minor, gray-green leaves that are fragrant when crushed. The plant produces tiny, yellow flowers that bloom in the fall. *California Goldenrod* (*Solidago velutina*) has tall, yellow flower clusters that resemble those of Coastal Tarweed. California goldenrod grows up to 6 feet tall and has green leaves that are lance-shaped and toothed.

Cautions: Coast Tarweed is not toxic, but the plant's leaves and stems can cause skin irritation due to the sticky hairs.

Culinary Preparation: The seed oil of this plant has been used in cooking as a substitute for olive oil. Women harvested coast tarweed seeds over a fortnight in late summer. Gathering the seeds was done with a seed beater and a basket. A bedrock mortar and stone pestle were used for winnowing and grinding the seeds. Winnowing and sifting were carried out in a circular basket plaque. The plaque was jiggled until the large fragments separated from the fine meal. A dry meal was prepared from large pieces ground into a fine powder—every household stored seed eaten throughout the year.

Medicinal Properties: Coast Tarweed has been used in traditional medicine to treat various ailments, including digestive and respiratory issues.

Fun Fact: The tar-like resin produced by Coast Tarweed is used by the larvae of some species of moths as a food source.

Dog Toxicity: Coast Tarweed is not known to be toxic to dogs.

Curly Dock
Rumex crispus [ROO-mex KRIHS-pus]

Because dock plants persist throughout the year, they can be collected for foraging all year. All parts of the plant are edible or medicinal, including the leaves, stem, seeds, and roots. Docks are members of the **Polygonaceae** (buckwheat) family and are commonly known as Yellow Docks, Yaller Docks, Sour Docks, Narrowleaf Docks, and Curled Docks.

Location: The curly dock can grow wild in disturbed areas, on roadsides, and along streams and ditches in temperate regions worldwide.

Identification:

GROWTH / SIZE:: a tall, upright plant that can grow up to 4 feet tall.

BARK / STEM / ROOT: The stem is smooth and green with red spots.

LEAF: Long, green, and curly-edged.

FLOWER: Yellow, small, and in clusters at the top of the stem.

FRUIT / SEED / NUT: Produces a seedhead with brown, curled seed pods that persist into the winter.

Look-a-like(s): *Broadleaf dock* (*Rumex obtusifolius*) is similar in many ways, but its leaves are broader and less curly. The seed heads are also smaller and less dense.

Common sorrel (*Rumex acetosa*) has smaller and less curly arrow-shaped leaves. The leaves of *Sheep sorrel* (*Rumex acetosella*) are usually smaller and more pointed, and the plant has a reddish stem.

Cautions: The leaves and stems of docks contain oxalic acid, which gives them their delicious sour flavor. Oxalic acid, however, hinders the absorption of minerals such as calcium and iron. Rhubarb, spinach, and Swiss chard also contain the compound. So as long as you don't consume excessive amounts of foods containing oxalic acid, your health will be fine.

Culinary preparation: Early spring is the best time to find dock leaves. The early harvest is generally sweeter and more tender. You can eat the dock leaves raw or cooked. When the plant grows a stem, it's too late. That stem implies that its basal leaves will be tough and bitter. While its stem leaves may be edible, the stem itself is the best. Harvest dock stems in late spring and early summer before they reach full height and flower. You should be able to flex and bend it; if not, it's too tough to eat. It may be stringy on the outside, but it can be peeled. Raw is best, but steamed or sautéed is just as delicious. Pickled is even an option.

Medicinal Properties: Curly Dock has a long history of use in traditional medicine, particularly for digestive issues and skin conditions. Chemicals contained in yellow dock work as laxatives and anti-inflammatory agents. Also, it contains chemicals that may kill parasites, bacteria, and fungi. Additionally, it has been used to treat pain, nasal passage swelling, constipation, hemorrhoids, and many other conditions.

Fun fact: The scientific name, Rumex, is derived from the Latin word "rumen," meaning "to chew," which refers to the plant's tough, fibrous leaves.

Dog toxicity: Dock is poisonous for dogs. The most common symptoms are drooling, loss of appetite, and trembling. Left untreated can lead to kidney failure, coma, and possible death.

F ourwing Saltbush

Atriplex canescens [A-TRUH-PLEKS KUH-NES-UHNS]

This species belongs to the **Chenopodiaceae** (Goosefoot) family and is commonly known as Chamiso or Chamisa.

Location: It grows wild in arid and semi-arid regions of North America, including deserts, plains, and sagebrush communities.

Identification:

GROWTH/SIZE: The most common size is 2 to 4 feet, but it can be as high as 10 feet. Depending on the climate, they can be evergreen or winter-deciduous.

BARK/STEM/ROOT: The bark is thin and tight, with heavy branching. It has rigid, brittle stems and is erect and round. In some cases, lateral branches are armed with spines at the tips. There are two types of roots in the plant's root system: a taproot and one or more lateral feeder roots found in higher soil layers. In southern California deserts, fourwing saltbush taproots can reach 40 feet deep.

LEAF: Gray-green, hairy, and triangular leaves range in length from 0.5 to 2 inches. Scales protect young leaves from water loss. There are hairlike epidermal outgrowths on mature leaves.

FLOWER: It has dense spikes of small, green to yellow staminate flowers 2 to 3 mm in width and panicles of pistillate flowers 2 to 16 inches long.

Fruit/seed/nut: The fruits are the only ones with four large wings in the genus. It blooms from April to July, producing tiny, triangular seeds in clusters that persist into the winter.

Look-a-like(s): *Shadscale* (*Atriplex confertifolia*) is a shrub with gray-green leaves and small flowers. Its leaves are more closely spaced, and smaller, and Shadscale is found in drier, more desert-like environments. *Winterfat* (*Krascheninnikovia lanata*) has silvery-gray leaves and small, inconspicuous flowers. The leaves are typically longer and narrower.

Cautions: When planted in selenium-rich soils, saltbush will accumulate high selenium levels. Chronic selenium poisoning can develop in animals that eat it. So it is essential to consult an expert before using the plant for animal feed.

Culinary Preparation: Fourwing Saltbush can be harvested for its edible leaves and seeds that have a salty flavor. The leaves can be harvested at any time during the growing season, and the seeds can be harvested in the fall when they are mature and dry. The seeds can be ground into a powder, mixed with cereals, used in cakes or piñole, or mixed with water to make a refreshing drink. Saltbush leaves have a salty, herbal flavor and are very versatile. The mildest flavor comes from young leaves. Toss fresh leaves into salads, stir-fries, dip them in batter, and fry them, or use the dried ones as a seasoning; ground dried leaves can be substituted for salt.

Medicinal Properties: Makes a soapy lather from the leaves and washes away itches and rashes such as chickenpox. You can reduce pain and swelling from ant bites by applying a poultice of crushed leaves.

Fun fact: Fourwing Saltbush is an important food source for many wildlife species, including pronghorns, mule deer, and birds.

Dog toxicity: Fourwing Saltbush is not considered toxic to dogs.

Giant Reed
Arundo donax [UH-RUN-DOH DON-AKS]

It was introduced in California in the 1820s for erosion control, but it escaped and has become a significant invasive weed in California watersheds. It belongs to the **Poaceae** (grass) family and has several common names, including giant cane, elephant grass, Spanish cane, Colorado river reed, and wild cane.

Location: These plants thrive in moist soil, dunes, wetlands, and riparian areas. They are found in streambanks, desert springs, flood plains, drainages, and irrigation waterways.

Identification:

GROWTH / SIZE: Giant reeds are large, clumping, perennial grasses with hollow stems 1/4 to 2 inches thick. Bamboo-like stems grow over 20 feet tall. The average height of a mature stand is 12 to 16 feet.

BARK / STEM / ROOT: The underground portion comprises an extensive network of light brown rhizomes and fibrous tap roots.

LEAF: Their mature size is about 2 inches wide by 24 to 36 inches long. An alternate arrangement of stiff or upright leaves is typical. Their surfaces are smooth, their bases are rounded, and they taper to an extended point. Leaf color can range from pale green to blue-green; the leaf's lower part is yellow, has fine hairs, and the stem is clasped in an S shape with tiny hairs along the margin; the ligules are large and papery.

Flower: The inflorescence is an erect feathery spike 1 to 2 feet long, ranging from whitish to brown, depending on maturity. Spikelets are stalked and solitary; the flowers have long, silky awns. The flowers bloom from June through November, depending on location.

Fruit/seed/nut: Although it can produce seeds under some conditions, there is no evidence that the seeds are viable.

Look-a-like(s): *Bamboo* (*Bambusa vulgaris*)

Cautions: None known other than the plant is invasive.

Culinary preparation: The rhizome can be eaten raw or cooked. It can be dried and ground into a powder to make bread, usually with cereal flour, or it can be roasted or boiled. The young leaves can be cooked and used as a potherb. The mature leaves are very bitter.

Medicinal properties: Dried leaves can be brewed with tea to stimulate appetite, stop vomiting, and relieve muscle aches, pains, and stiffness. The root is a diuretic for urine purification, gonorrhea, itchy skin, and menstrual flow stimulation. When boiled in wine with honey, the root or rhizome has been used for treating cancer.

Fun fact: Flute makers in ancient Greece made flutes with the cane, known as kala-maulos, or "cane flutes." Due to their high silica content, these canes are durable and can be used to make fishing rods and walking sticks.

Dog toxicity: Despite not being considered poisonous to pets, the alkaloid gramine is toxic to various animals. As a vasopressor, it is stated to raise blood pressure in dogs after small doses and cause it to fall after larger quantities.

Goosegrass
Galium aparine [GAY-lee-um ap-uh-REE-nee]

A California native, common names include common bedstraw, common cleavers, common clivers, goosegrass, catchweed, sticky weed, robin-run-the-hedge, sticky willy, sticky willow, velcro weed, and grip grass. It is an annual herbaceous plant belonging to the **Rubiaceae** (bedstraw) family. Because of the presence of small prickles on the stems and leaves, the herbage sticks to clothing and animal fur. With these prickles, the plant can crawl over other plants and compete with them for sunlight.

Location: Its habitats include coniferous forests, deciduous woodlands, meadows, prairies, flood plains, disturbed areas, abandoned fields, and cultivated crops.

Identification:

GROWTH / SIZE: Goosegrass is easily identified by its whitish, flattened stem and prostrate growth habit. The plant grows half an inch to 2 feet tall.

BARK / STEM / ROOT: Many stems grow from one common root in a bunch or rosette. The base of the weed is silver or gray.

LEAF: The leaves are flat or slightly folded and dark green. Near the base, stems are often hairy or tufted; further out in the plant, they become smooth.

FLOWER: Typically, there are two to five racemes per inflorescence, with the seeds arranged herringbone style. The white flowers have four petals each and bloom in the late summer and early fall.

FRUIT / SEED / NUT: Small, brown seeds are produced in the seed heads. Seeds at the end of the leaves look like a zipper.

Look-a-like(s): Because of its finger-like spikes and growth habit, goosegrass superficially resembles *Crabgrasses* (*Digitaria spp.*). Crabgrass has dull foliage, while goosegrass has shiny foliage. Crabgrass has finger-like spikes that are narrower than goosegrass, usually green or reddish-green, and less shiny.

Cautions: Occasionally, it causes a localized rash known as contact dermatitis on people's skin.

Culinary preparation: When gathered before the fruits appear, the plant's leaves and stems can be cooked as a leaf vegetable. While the plant is edible raw, the numerous small hooks that cover it and give it its clinging nature can make it unpleasant to eat. Most commonly, tea is made from dried leaves. You can either brew it hot or cold. Cold infusion can be refrigerated in cold water for 24–48 hours. Often, goosegrass fruits are dried, roasted, and used as a caffeine-free substitute for coffee.

Medicinal properties: Traditionally, cleavers were used to make poultices and washes for treating skin ailments, wounds, and burns. Scurvy, psoriasis, eczema, seborrhea, sunburn, freckles, sores, blisters, injuries, and burns have been traditionally treated with this remedy.

Fun fact: Cleavers' barbed stems could be used to make a "rough sieve" for straining milk by ancient Greek shepherds. In Europe, several bedstraws were used to maintain a uniform thickness of the bed filling because the clinging hairs caused the branches to stick together. Cleaver roots can be used to create a permanent red dye.

Dog toxicity: Goosegrass is safe for dogs. The antioxidants, minerals, and other nutrients make it particularly beneficial. It is also rich in vitamin C and silica, both beneficial to teeth and bones. The lymphatic system, skin, and hair benefit from fatty acids, flavonoids, and tannins. In addition, goosegrass is an effective diuretic that helps your dog eliminate waste from his system and increases urine output.

L amb's Quarters
Chenopodium album [KEH-NOH-POH-DEE-UM AL-BUHM]

Goosefoot or Lamb's quarter is a highly adaptable and nutritious annual edible in the **Amaranthaceae** (buckwheat) family. Leaf shapes resemble goose's feet, hence the common name. This plant has several other common names, including Melde, wild spinach, Baconweed, Fat Hen, Frost-blite, and Pigweed.

Location: Lambs' quarters can grow wild in various habitats, including fields, gardens, waste places, and streams and rivers' edges. It is commonly found throughout temperate regions of the world.

Identification:

GROWTH / SIZE: it's an herbaceous annual that can reach up to 6 feet tall.

BARK / STEM / ROOT: The stem is erect, branching, and smooth, with a diameter of about 0.5 inches. The roots are long and shallow, reaching a depth of 18 inches, and can grow up to 24 inches long.

LEAF: are alternate, simple, and triangular to diamond-shaped, with toothed margins. They are typically 1-4 inches long and 1-3 inches wide. The upper surface of the leaves is green, while the lower surface is pale green. The leaves are covered in a white, powdery substance, giving them a slightly fuzzy appearance.

FLOWER: are small and arranged in dense clusters called panicles. The flowers are green to yellow-green and lack petals, sepals, and nectar-producing structures. The male and female flowers are usually found on separate plants.

FRUIT / SEED / NUT: The seed is tiny, round, flat, and about 1/16 to 1/8 inch in diameter. The seeds are enclosed in a papery, bladder-like covering that is easy to remove. When ripe, the seeds are black and shiny and can be easily dispersed by wind. They have a high germination rate and can remain viable in the soil for up to 40 years.

Look-a-like(s): *Black nightshade* (*Solanum nigrum*) is often miscategorized as poisonous. It is edible but does require more caution than lamb's quarters. *Orache* (*Atriplex hortensis*) can look very similar to lamb quarters. Since lamb's quarters and orache are variable plants, the best way to distinguish them is by the flowers and seeds. Lamb's quarter's flowers are rounded or oval, while the female flowers of orache have two triangular- or diamond-shaped bracteoles.

Cautions: While it does not pose a health risk to humans, it does contain saponins and oxalic acid. Some individuals may experience an allergic reaction to Lambs' quarter. Eating in large quantities can cause digestive upset and disturb the nervous system.

Culinary preparation: Lamb's quarter can be used as a cooked green, similar to spinach, in various dishes, including soups, stews, and stir-fries. You can eat raw or cooked leaves as a leaf vegetable, but moderate consumption is recommended due to high oxalic acid levels. It is also possible to cook flower buds and flowers. It produces tens of thousands of black seeds per plant, also edible after roasting or boiling.

Medicinal properties: Lamb's quarter has a long history of use in traditional medicine, particularly as a tonic and blood purifier. It is said to help support healthy skin and urinary function and to help regulate blood sugar levels.

Fun fact: Lamb's quarter is a relative of the cultivated grain quinoa.

Dog toxicity: Lamb's quarter is not considered toxic to dogs.

Marsh Labrador Tea

Rhododendron tomentosum [ROW-DOH-DEN-dron TOH-MEN-TOH-SUM]

If Labrador tea is used in concentrated solutions or large amounts, it is LIKELY UNSAFE.

Native Americans used Labrador Tea extensively to treat asthma, rheumatism, burns, and liver and kidney ailments. It belongs to the **Ericaceae** (heather) family. It is also known as Bog Labrador Tea, Muskeg Tea, Indian Tea, James Tea, Marsh Tea, and Swamp Tea.

Location: Labrador tea is found in wetlands, bogs, damp and dry woods, ponds, exposed areas, and arctic-alpine barrens.

Identification:

GROWTH/SIZE: This shrub is low to medium-sized and can grow from 19 1/2 inches to 40 inches tall, though it is usually much shorter.

BARK/STEM/ROOT: The bark is coppery-orange to reddish brown. There is a dense covering of hairs on the twigs, and it has upright stems. In the first year, new branches are covered with coppery hairs, which eventually gray out and persist for many years. Older wood has gray bark.

LEAF: A cluster of oblong, blunt, or tapered leaves covers the upper branches. A single leaf is attached to each plant node in an alternate pattern. Each leaf has smooth edges that turn down. Its thick, leathery leaves range from 1 to 2 1/4 inches long and 1/4 to 2/3 inches wide. The top of the leaves are glossy and green, and a dense mat of tangled woolly hair covers its lower surface. The hair is white on young leaves but rusty orange or brown on mature leaves. Early spring to September is the best time to collect leaves. To avoid harming the plants, only take a few leaves from each one.

FLOWER: Approximately ten to forty tiny white flowers are produced in rounded clusters in late spring. The clusters at the ends of the stem are generally 1.5 to 2.5 inches wide. Flower clusters measure about half an inch across and contain five petals and five to ten slender stamens around a small, round green ovary.

FRUIT / SEED / NUT: Brown septicidal capsules are produced by the shrub in the summer.

Look-a-like(s): *Dwarf Labrador tea* (*Rhododendron groenlandicum*) is a similar but smaller species with narrower leaves.

Cautions: *Sheep laurel* (*Kalmia angustifolia*), or goowiddy, looks similar and is toxic. Identify it by its hairless leaves and stems, green underside to leaves, and pink flowers.

Culinary preparation: Labrador tea leaves can be made into a tea and served hot or iced. It has a floral flavor and is caffeine free.

Medicinal properties: Among the many medicinal uses for the leaves are chest ailments such as sore throats, chest congestion, coughs, and lung infections. It can also be used for diarrhea, kidney problems, rheumatism, and headaches. In the past, women have used it to cause abortion or added it to bath water to help ease skin issues.

Fun Fact: The spicy leaves of Labrador Tea have been used to make a tasty herbal tea for centuries. Infusions of this plant, for example, were used by the Algonquin to treat headaches and colds. The Chippewa used powdered roots to treat burns and ulcers. A poultice made from the leaves was applied to wounds by the Cree to treat insect sting pain and rheumatism. The Oweekeno used an infusion of leaves for treating sore throats.

Dog Toxicity: This one is toxic to your pup. If eaten, symptoms can occur, such as vomiting, diarrhea, abdominal pain, abnormal heart rate, heart arrhythmias, weakness, tremors, transient blindness, seizures, and coma.

M iner's Lettuce
Claytonia perfoliata [KLAY-TOH-NEE-UH PER-FUH-LEE-AY-TUH]

A flowering plant in the **Montiaceae** (miner lettuce) family. It's also known as Indian lettuce, winter purslane, or by the Cahuilla Indian tribe name, palsingat. Its name refers to how gold miners used the plant during the California Gold Rush, eating it to prevent scurvy.

Location: Northern San Joaquin Valley and Sacramento region are the most common areas for this species. Disturbed and wasteland, moist banks, and slopes, especially in partial shade, are usually the habitats of this plant.

Identification:

GROWTH/SIZE: This tender rosette grows up to 12 inches tall, resembling mini lily pads.

BARK/STEM/ROOT: The stem appears to pass directly through the center of the round or kidney-shaped leaves. It's usually green or reddish and can reach up to 12 inches tall. Typically smooth and hairless, it's pretty thin and delicate, but also quite strong and flexible, which allows it to support the weight of the leaves and flowers.

LEAF: Typically, the first true leaves form a rosette at the base of the plant and measure from 1/4 to 1 5/8 inches in length with an 8-inch petiole. Usually, the plant appears after heavy rains in sunlit areas. The leaves turn red as they dry out as the days get hotter and drier.

FLOWER: From February to June, the flowers appear in groups of 5–40. Five petals on the small pink or white flowers measure between 1/16 and 1/4 inches. Flower buds grow above a pair of leaves connected around the stem to form a single circular leaf. As the plants mature, they form a rosette, with numerous erect to spreading stems.

FRUIT/SEED/NUT: The seeds are small, round, and flattened, approximately 1-2 mm. Usually black or dark brown and have a shiny, smooth surface. They are produced in small, elongated capsules about 5-10 mm long. When mature, the capsules split open along a central line, releasing the small seeds.

Look-a-like(s): *Dollarweed* (*Hydrocotyle umbellata*) produces clusters of small white flowers on separate stems rather than in the center of the leaf itself.

Cautions: It is crucial not to over-harvest Miner's lettuce when foraging in the wild because it will not reseed.

Culinary preparation: You can remove a few leaves by pinching near the soil at the base of the stem, don't pull. Always leave a handful of leaves behind to ensure each plant can photosynthesize and grow. The entire plant, except for the roots, is edible and a good source of vitamin C. Most often, it is eaten raw in salads. Occasionally, it is boiled like spinach, which has a similar taste.

Medicinal properties: The leaves have long been used as a gentle laxative, invigorating spring tonic, and diuretic by herbalists. Like aloe vera gel, it has a soothing and cooling effect when applied topically. Poultices from the leaves can treat burns, minor skin irritations, and inflamed or painful joints.

Fun Fact: The seeds are dispersed by ants, which are attracted to an elaiosome attached to the seed. The ants carry the seeds back to their nests, feeding on the elaiosome and discarding the seed, which may then germinate and grow into a new plant.

Dog Toxicity: none known

S carlet Pimpernel
Anagallis aravensis [UH-NUH-GAL-ISS AR-VEN-SIS]

Traditionally included in the **Primulaceae** (primrose) family, humans have distributed the species widely, deliberately as an ornamental flower, or accidentally. It's now naturalized almost worldwide. It's commonly known as red pimpernel, red chickweed, poor man's barometer, poor man's weather glass, shepherd's weather glass, or shepherd's clock.

Location: They require moist soil but do not tolerate waterlogging. There are many places where they can be found, including crop fields, pastures, grasslands, turf, gardens, landscaped areas, urban sites, roadside margins, streams, marshes, ocean beaches, disturbed and waste ground, and fields.

Identification:

GROWTH / SIZE: It typically grows 2-12 inches tall and spreads to form a dense mat.

BARK / STEM / ROOT: The stems are usually ascending and are covered in fine hairs. The roots are shallow and fibrous.

LEAF: The leaves are oval to oblong, with a smooth margin and a slightly rough texture. They are typically 2-5 cm long and 1-2 cm wide and are arranged opposite each other on the stem.

FLOWER: The flowers are small, with five petals that are typically bright scarlet but can also be pink, blue, or white. They are solitary or arranged in loose clusters and bloom from spring to autumn.

FRUIT/NUT/SEED: The seeds are produced in small, flattened capsules at the end of the stems. The capsules contain several seeds that are usually dispersed when they split open.

Look-alike Plants: none noted

Cautions: It contains toxic saponins and cytotoxic cucurbitacins, so it is no longer recommended for internal use. Although the seeds can poison some mammals, no human cases have been reported. Some people may develop dermatitis after coming into contact with the plant.

Culinary Preparation: Flowers bloom from May until the end of August. If you gather the whole herb in June when the leaves are at their best, you can use it fresh or dried. There is no odor to pimpernel, but it has a bitter, astringent taste.

Medicinal Uses: Scarlet Pimpernel has kept its ancient reputation, especially in treating brain diseases. Herbal decoctions or tinctures have been used in treating melancholy and related mental disorders. The whole plant, dried and powdered, is excellent for treating epilepsy, and there are numerous well-authenticated accounts of it completely curing the disease. In addition, the flowers alone have been found helpful in treating epilepsy.

Fun Fact: In the Middle Ages, the plant was also thought to have magical properties and was associated with the devil. Picking the plant on a particular day was believed to bring bad luck or even death.

Dog Toxicity: It's considered toxic to pets. The plant contains several poisonous compounds that can cause digestive upset, including vomiting and diarrhea, as well as more serious symptoms such as tremors, seizures, and even death in severe cases.

Seacoast Angelica

Angelica lucida [AN-JUH-LIK-UH LOO-SID-UH]

Known for attracting bees and butterflies, this herb belongs to the **Apiaceae** (Carrot) family and is native to North America. In addition to being known as Sea-watch, it is often confused with several other similar species in the same family and mistakenly called wild celery.

Location: They're on coastal bluffs, beaches, and estuaries along Northern California, the Pacific Northwest, and Alaska coastlines.

Identification:

GROWTH / SIZE: It can reach a height of 2-6 feet, with a spread of 1-2 feet.

BARK / STEM / ROOT: The stem is green, round, and hollow and can grow up to 3 inches in diameter. The roots are fibrous and can reach a length of several feet.

LEAF: The leaves are large, pinnate, and can reach 12 inches long. They are bright green and have a glossy appearance.

FLOWER: The flowers are small and white, growing in clusters, and can reach up to 1 inch in diameter. They are arranged in large, umbrella-like clusters that can reach up to 6 inches in diameter.

FRUIT / SEED / NUT: The fruit is a small, dry, one-seeded *schizocarp* less than 1/4 inch in diameter. The seeds are tiny and have a slightly flattened shape.

Look-a-like(s): *Purple Angelica* (*Angelica atropurpurea*) has purple stems and slightly smaller leaves. Some people may be allergic, so monitoring your body's reaction is essential if you consume it. *Sweet Cicely* (*Osmorhiza chilensis*) has a more delicate appearance and a less robust stem. The leaves and seeds of sweet cicely have a lovely, licorice-like flavor and are commonly used as a seasoning or to make tea. However, it is essential to note that some people may be allergic to sweet cicely, which should be used cautiously. Additionally, consuming the plant in small amounts is recommended, as overconsumption may cause digestive upset or other adverse effects.

Cautions: *Cow Parsnip* (*Heracleum lanatum*) has large, white, umbrella-like flower clusters and a much thicker stem. It contains a phototoxic compound called furanocoumarin, which can cause skin irritation, rashes, and blistering when the plant is touched and exposed to sunlight. In addition to skin irritation, consuming large amounts of cow parsnip can cause digestive upset, including nausea, vomiting, and diarrhea.

Culinary preparation: The young leaves can be chopped and added to salads for a slightly bitter flavor and a crisp texture. The young stems can be sliced and stir-fried with other vegetables for a unique flavor. They can also be pickled for a tangy and crunchy snack. The leaves and stems can be dried and used to make tea.

Medicinal properties: An infusion can be made by steeping the leaves in boiling water to make tea. The tea can treat various ailments, including digestive issues, colds and flu, and skin conditions. Tinctures are often used to treat digestive issues and as a tonic to boost overall health. An ointment can be applied topically to treat skin conditions such as rashes, cuts, and burns. Angelica lucida essential oil can be used in aromatherapy to treat various ailments, including anxiety, stress, and insomnia.

Fun Fact: It is important to note that it is a protected species in some states, and collecting or harvesting the plant without permission is illegal.

Dog Toxicity: it's not known to be toxic to dogs.

S owthistle

Sonchus oleraceus [SAHN-KUHS OH-LUH-RAY-SEE-UHS]

This plant grows year-round in California's Central Valley and coastal areas, where it is abundant. It belongs to the **Asteraceae** (aster) family, and its common names include Creeping Sow Thistle, Dindle, Gutweed, Milk Thistle, and Tree Sow-thistle.

Location: Agricultural land and disturbed areas are home to annual sowthistle plants that are widespread in winter or summer.

Identification:

GROWTH / SIZE: This herbaceous annual or biennial plant can grow 2 to 5 feet tall.

BARK / STEM / ROOT: The stem is smooth and fleshy, with a diameter of about 0.5 inches. The root system is fibrous and shallow.

LEAF: The leaves are alternate and have a rosette shape, 4 to 12 inches in diameter. They are green and have a slightly waxy texture. The leaves are deeply lobed, with jagged edges and a prickly texture.

FLOWER: The flowers are yellow, with a diameter of about 1 inch. They are arranged in a composite inflorescence 2 to 3 inches in diameter. The flowers are arranged in a circular pattern on the end of a stem, and they bloom from spring to autumn.

FRUIT / SEED / NUT: The seed is an achene, a small, dry, one-seeded fruit that does not split open. The achenes are about 0.1 to 0.2 inches long and are dispersed by the wind.

Look-a-like(s): *Dandelion* (*Taraxacum officinale*) Many people confuse sow thistle with dandelions, but dandelion only has one flower per stalk, and the leaves grow at the base of the plant. *Rough Hawkbit* (Leontodon hispidus), the leaves are less deeply lobed, and the flowers are smaller.

Cautions: *Prickly Lettuce* (*Lactuca serriola*) has deeply lobed leaves with a prickly texture and yellow flowers arranged in a composite inflorescence. Ingesting large amounts can cause dizziness, headache, nausea, and vomiting.

Culinary preparation: Young leaves and stems can be eaten raw in salads, providing a slightly bitter flavor, or added to stir-fry. Older leaves, like spinach or Swiss chard, can be boiled and served as a cooked green. It can be added to soups and stews to flavor or substitute for other greens like spinach or kale. The leaves can be chopped and used to make a pesto sauce, either on their own or in combination with other herbs and nuts.

Medicinal properties: Tea infusions have been used as a diuretic to help increase urine production and flush out toxins from the body. Poultices have been used to help relieve pain and swelling from injuries and infections. Decoctions have been used to treat digestive disorders and help regulate the menstrual cycle.

Fun Fact: The plant's bright yellow flowers are a significant source of nectar for pollinators, and its seeds are a valuable food source for birds and other seed-eating animals.

Dog Toxicity: Generally, milk thistle is regarded as safe for dogs, but different doses may be recommended depending on the problem being treated. The general recommendation for detoxing your dog is 1-2 mg per pound to prevent harmful build-up and support liver function. You can perform the detox once or twice a year for 3-6 weeks to remove any toxic build-up and maintain the health of your pup's liver.

S tinging Nettle
Urtica dioica [YOOR-TIH-KUH DEE-OH-IH-KUH]

There are many different names for nettles. They are commonly known as common nettle, burn nettle, stinging nettle, or just nettle leaves. Stinging Nettle is a member of the **Urticaceae** (nettles) family with perennial flowering stems.

Location: Waste ground, hedgerows, woods, etc., can be used to grow this plant. It prefers moist soil and can tolerate strong winds.

Identification:

GROWTH/SIZE: it can grow up to 4 feet tall but typically ranges from 2 to 3 feet.

BARK/STEM/ROOT: The plant's stem is upright, square-shaped, and covered with stinging hairs that can cause skin irritation upon contact. The roots are shallow and spread out to form a dense rhizome network, allowing the plant to form large colonies.

LEAF: The leaves are opposite, ovate, and can grow up to 6 inches long and 4 inches wide. They have serrated edges and are covered with stinging hairs, which protect the plant from herbivores.

FLOWER: The flowers are small, green, and arranged in dense clusters. The inflorescences are usually drooping and can grow up to 6 inches long.

Fruit/seed/nut: After fertilizing the flowers, they produce small, greenish-brown fruits about 1/16 inch in diameter. The fruits contain tiny seeds dispersed by wind and can remain viable in the soil for several years.

Look-a-like(s): The *White dead-nettle* (*Lamium album*), *Dwarf nettle* (*Urtica urens*), *Canadian wood nettle* (*Laportea Canadensis*), *Clearweed* (*Pilea pumila*), and *False nettle* (*Boehmeria cylindrica*) are all plants that look similar to stinging nettle, but are different in that they do not have any stinging hairs.

Cautions: it can cause skin dermatitis when touched due to the spines, be sure to wear gloves when harvesting.

Culinary preparation: It is in leaf from March to November, in flower from May to October, and the seeds ripen from June to October. The nettle leaves can be used to prepare polenta, pesto, and purée, among other recipes. Young shoots should be soaked in warm water to remove dirt and debris. Cook young shoots in salted boiling water for five minutes. It can be eaten as a vegetable or added to soups. Once cooked, the stinging sensation disappears.

Medicinal properties: Many forms of stinging nettle are available, including teas, tinctures, fluid extracts, and creams. Today's most common use is managing urinary problems during an enlarged prostate's early stages. In addition to treating urinary tract infections and hay fever, it treats joint pain, sprains and strains, tendonitis, and insect bites. This is done in the form of compresses or creams.

Fun Fact: The broad-leaf dock (*Rumex obtusifolius*) often grows in similar environments as stinging nettles and is viewed as a folk remedy for counteracting their sting.

Dog Toxicity: Even primary contact with this plant can affect dogs. Symptoms include redness, swelling, and itching. Ingestion of stinging nettle can cause profuse salivation, mouth pawing, vomiting, labored breathing, twitching, and ataxia. Fortunately, most stinging nettle poisoning results only in dermatitis. A warm bath and topical anti-histamine medication can relieve itching and redness.

Woolly Blue Curls

Trichostema lanceolatum [TRI-KOH-STEM-UH LAN-SEE-OH-LAY-TUHM]

This plant is native to California and belongs to the **Lamiaceae** (mint) family. Its other names are Rosemary, Blue-curls, Camphor weed, yerba del aigre, stinkweed, turpentine weed, wild rosemary, and vinegarweed.

Location: A significant component of coastal sage scrub, chaparral, and oak woodland communities, it grows near creek beds and bottomlands with more moist soil.

Identification:

GROWTH / SIZE: it's a small perennial herb that grows up to 1-3 feet tall and 1-2 feet wide.

BARK / STEM / ROOT: The stem is erect, slender, and often branching. It is covered with short, stiff hairs and has a woody base that becomes brown with age. The stem is about 0.1-0.2 inches in diameter.

LEAF: The leaves are linear or lanceolate, up to 1 inch long and 0.1-0.3 inches wide. They are alternate, sessile, and usually covered with short, stiff hairs. The margins are smooth or slightly toothed, and the tip is pointed.

FLOWER: The flowers are small, tubular, and blue to lavender. They are arranged in clusters at the end of the stems, and each flower is about 0.3-0.4 inches long and 0.2-

0.3 inches wide. The flowers have a strong fragrance, resembling the smell of vinegar, which gives the plant its common name.

Fruit/seed/nut: The fruit is a small, four-chambered capsule that contains four tiny, black, shiny seeds. Each seed is about 0.08-0.12 inches long and 0.04-0.06 inches wide.

Look-a-like(s): Several plants look similar to Woolly Blue Curls, though none are edible. Here a just a few of the most common. *Wild Lantana* (*Lantana involucrata*) produces small clusters of flowers similar in color to vinegarweed. *Desert Lavender* (*Hyptis emoryi*) has clusters of small purple flowers that are similar in shape.

Cautions: Some people may experience skin irritation or allergic reactions when handling the plant.

Culinary preparation: Vinegarweed can flavor oils, such as olive oil; wash and dry the leaves and add them to a clean glass jar with the olive oil. Allow the mixture to sit for several days, strain out the leaves, and use the infused oil in dressings or cooking oil. Chop up the fresh leaves and use them as a substitute for vinegar in recipes, such as salad dressings, marinades, and sauces. It can be used in herb blends, chopping the fresh leaves and mixing them with other herbs, such as thyme, rosemary, and oregano.

Medicinal properties: For stomach upset and menstrual cramps, the dried flowers and leaves are stripped off and used to make tea. An ointment made from fresh flowers/leaves can treat bruises. Colds, stomachaches, headaches, ague, bladder problems, and malaria were treated with a decoction or tea from the leaves and flowers. Gargling vinegarweed tea treated throat inflammation. A hot infusion was sniffed into the nasal passages to treat colds, coughs, headaches, and nosebleeds.

Fun Fact: They tend to have a short lifespan since they follow the fire. For seeds to germinate, they need a chemical stimulus from the burning Coastal Sage Scrub or Chaparral smoke.

Dog Toxicity: This plant is not toxic to your pup. It can be used as a flea repellant; the leaves and stems of the plant are crushed and placed inside the bedding.

Yellow Monkey Flower

Erythranthe guttata [AIR-UH-THRAN-THEE GUT-TAY-TUH]

This plant is named after the similarity between its blooms and the face of a monkey. It belongs to the **Scrophulariaceae** (figwort) family. Common names are Golden Monkeyflower, Seep Monkeyflower, and Common Monkeyflower.

Location: Monkey flowers grow in seeps, springs, or along creeks. The roots often trail right into the surface of ponds and streams. It is common for some plants to have their roots in shallow water.

Identification:

GROWTH / SIZE: a perennial herbaceous plant growing up to 3 feet tall.

BARK / STEM / ROOT: Its stem is erect and branching, with a diameter of about 0.1 inches. The root system is fibrous and shallow, extending only a few inches into the soil.

LEAF: The leaves are simple, alternate, and ovate. They range from 0.5 to 2.5 inches long and 0.25 to 1 inch wide. The leaves are green and slightly hairy, with serrated edges.

FLOWER: The flowers are trumpet-shaped and yellow, with red dots on the flower's lower lip. They are about 3/4 inches long and 1 inch wide. The flowers are produced in clusters at the ends of the stems and bloom from late spring to early fall.

FRUIT/SEED/NUT: The fruit is a capsule that contains numerous tiny seeds. The capsule is about 1/4 inch long and 1/10 inch wide. The seeds are small and dark brown.

Look-a-like(s) Because there are several species of monkeyflower, several look-a-likes appear, but all are edible.

Cautions: The plant contains toxic substances, such as iridoids and glycosides, which can cause skin irritation, vomiting, and diarrhea.

Culinary preparation: Though not recommended for consumption, the leaves can be added to salads as a lettuce substitute.

Medicinal properties: Although not great for ingesting, it has various medicinal properties. It contains flavonoids and other compounds that may reduce inflammation. It contains compounds that inhibit the spread of harmful microorganisms. It promotes tissue regeneration and repair. It has been used to treat anxiety and depression symptoms due to its calming and mood-enhancing properties and is believed to have broncho-dilating effects.

Fun Fact: Monkey Flowers are yellow bee-pollinated wildflowers that grow along the banks of streams and seep throughout most of California. Hummingbirds are fond of it, which makes it an excellent plant for flower beds, and deer do not like it, making it a natural deterrent.

Dog Toxicity: Yes, it's toxic to dogs. The plant contains glycosides, which can cause vomiting, diarrhea, lethargy, loss of appetite, and other symptoms if ingested by dogs. In severe cases, it can cause cardiac arrhythmia and even death.

Yellow Nutsedge
Cyperus esculentus [SIGH-PEAR-US ESS-KEW-LENT-US]

The yellow nutsedge, known as chufa, tiger nut, atadwe, and earth almond, is a widespread **Cyperaceae** (sedge) family member.

Location: California has yellow nutsedge throughout the state, and it grows actively during the summer heat when cool-season turf grows slowly. In late April or May, yellow nutsedge typically emerges and continues to produce until the first frost in autumn.

Identification:

GROWTH/SIZE: a perennial plant that grows up to 3 feet tall and spreads via underground tubers.

BARK/STEM/ROOT: The triangular stem can grow up to 1/2 inch in diameter. It is green and sturdy, with short, brown sheath nodes. The root system is fibrous and shallow, with a root network that spreads horizontally. The tubers can be up to 1 inch long and 1/2 inch in diameter.

LEAF: The leaves are linear, with a V-shaped cross-section, and grow up to 20 inches long. They are arranged in a basal rosette, with a tuft of leaves at the top of the stem.

FLOWER: The flowers are small and arranged in a terminal cluster. A bunch of bracts longer than the inflorescence surrounds them.

FRUIT/SEED/NUT: the fruit is a small, nut-like achene up to 1/4 inch long.

Look-a-like(s): *Purple nutsedge* (*Cyperus rotundus*) has broader leaves, and the seed-head is more rounded. *Watergrass* (*Echinochloa crus-galli*) has seedheads that are smaller and more compact. *Green kyllinga* (*Kyllinga brevifolia*) has more delicate leaves, and the seedheads are smaller and more rounded.

Cautions: Some people may be allergic to yellow nutsedge, as it can produce pollen that can cause respiratory irritation.

Culinary preparation: Yellow nutsedge can be used to make a non-dairy milk alternative that is rich and creamy. It can be ground into a gluten-free flour that is high in fiber. The flour can be used in baking or as a thickener for soups and sauces. It's used to make a sweet, milky drink called horchata. Or it can be ground into a nut butter similar in texture to almond butter. Nut butter can be a spread or a base for sauces and dressings.

Medicinal properties: Yellow nutsedge has been traditionally used to help with digestion and relieve constipation. This may be due to its high fiber content, which can help to regulate bowel movements. It has been shown to have anti-inflammatory properties, which may make it helpful for conditions such as arthritis and other inflammatory diseases. It contains a prebiotic fiber that can help support healthy gut bacteria making it beneficial for overall digestive health. It also contains antioxidants that may help protect against oxidative stress and cell damage, making it useful for overall health and may help to prevent chronic diseases.

Fun Fact: In ancient Egypt, yellow nutsedge was considered a sacred food commonly used in religious ceremonies. It was even found in the tomb of Tutankhamun, the famous Egyptian pharaoh.

Dog Toxicity: not considered to be toxic to dogs. However, the nutsedge tubers can be a choking hazard if dogs eat them whole.

Yellow Rocketcress

Barbaraea vulgaris [BAR-BUH-REE-UH VUL-GAIR-ISS]

It is a leafy green that grows wild and can be cultivated in a home garden. It is a part of the **Brassicaceae** *(mustard) family*. Other names for this plant are American Cress, Upland Cress, Garden Cress, or Creasy Cress.

Location: It grows in cultivated and wasteland conditions, including fields, rocky outcrops, railroad embankments, and roadsides. While it does well in most soil types, it prefers moist, well-drained sandy to loamy soil.

Identification:

GROWTH / SIZE: a herbaceous plant that grows up to 24 inches tall.

BARK / STEM / ROOT: It has an erect stem that is often branched and can be up to 1/4 inch in diameter. The root system is shallow and fibrous.

LEAF: The leaves are alternate, lobed, and roughly oval-shaped, growing up to 3 inches long and 1.5 inches wide. The leaves have a slightly hairy texture and are a bright green color.

FLOWER: The flowers are bright yellow, with four petals arranged in a cross shape, and grow in clusters at the end of the stems. They are about 1/2 inches in diameter—the plant blooms from May to August.

FRUIT / SEED / NUT: The fruit is a long, narrow pod about 1 inch long and contains numerous tiny seeds. The seeds are oval-shaped and brown.

Look-a-like(s): *Hairy bittercress* (*Cardamine hirsuta*) has a similar rosette of lobed leaves and small white flowers. The flowers have only four petals, and the plant is much smaller. *Garlic mustard* (*Alliaria petiolata*) has similar toothed and lobed leaves. Its leaves are triangular, and it has a distinctive odor when crushed. *Shepherd's purse* (*Capsella bursa-pastoris*) has small white flowers and a rosette of lobed leaves. Seed pods, however, are triangular and much smaller.

Cautions: It may cause allergic reactions in some people. You should avoid consuming this plant if you are allergic to mustard or other cruciferous vegetables. Small amounts of toxic compounds known as glucosinolates may occur, though minuscule quantities are not harmful; large doses may cause digestive upset or other health problems.

Culinary preparation: Young leaves can be added to salads for a slightly bitter, peppery flavor. Mix them with lettuce, spinach, or arugula for a tasty salad. You can also sauté them with garlic and oil for a delicious side dish. To make a flavorful pesto, use the leaves instead of basil. Garnish savory dishes with flowers for a pretty and tasty presentation. Add a pop of color and flavor to soups, stews, and roasted vegetables with them. Last but not least, you can top sandwiches with leaves. They pair well with cheese, avocados, and roasted vegetables.

Medicinal properties: Anti-inflammatory compounds are present, helping relieve pain and inflammation associated with arthritis and rheumatism. Traditionally, it is used to treat digestive complaints such as indigestion and bloating. As a respiratory remedy, it relieves coughs and bronchitis, loosens mucus, and soothes the airways. Evidence shows it has antimicrobial activity against several strains of bacteria, such as Staphylococcus aureus and E. coli. It may help to prevent infections and support the immune system.

Fun Fact: During World War II, the British used it as a vegetable and dubbed it "the poor man's capers."

Dog Toxicity: This one is safe for your pups.

PAY IT FORWARD!

UNLOCK THE POWER OF NATURE'S GENEROSITY

"The greatest gifts are not wrapped in paper but in love and the beauty of nature." - Anonymous.

Picture this: someone's standing in the middle of the wilderness, surrounded by the raw beauty of nature. But there's a tiny hiccup - they're a tad unsure which of the green wonders before them might serve as a delicious snack or which might send them on an unplanned trip to the ER. Now, what if YOUR review could be the deciding factor that guides them on this journey? How many times have we relied on the experiences of others before diving into a new adventure? Countless, right? How gratifying does it feel when we can be that guiding light for someone else?

Leaving a review isn't just a simple clickety-clack of your keyboard. Nope! It's a chance to share your wisdom, your "Ah-ha!" moments, and even your "Oops, shouldn't have eaten that" tales. By jotting down your thoughts, you're crafting a lighthouse for fellow enthusiasts, helping them navigate the vast ocean of edible greens.

Why We Need YOU!

In this digital age, there's an overabundance of information, but what's truly precious? Genuine experiences. Your insights are invaluable. By leaving an honest review, you ensure others get the most out of their edible journey without the pitfalls. Remember, your words could be the compass someone else is desperately seeking.

We're reaching out with a heartfelt plea: could you spare a few moments to leave an honest review? Your words will be the torch that lights up another enthusiast's path.

How to Review:

Just scan the QR code below:

Pour your heart out! Let us know what you loved and learned and any tips you might have.

Hit "Submit," and voilà, the review is done! It only takes 30 seconds to help others benefit.

The Ripple Effect

Every keystroke, every word, creates a ripple. By sharing your experiences, you're not just adding to a digital platform but making a real, tangible impact in someone's life. Your review could catalyze someone's passion or help a novice avoid a potentially prickly situation.

Happy Foraging,

Shannon Warner

PART FIVE
NUTS ABOUT CALIFORNIA
FORAGING FOR WILD EDIBLE TREES AND NUTS

California Bay Laurel

Umbellularia californica [UM-BUH-SELL-YOO-REE-UH KÆ-LIH-FOR-NI-KUH]

The early settlers of the West gave this species the nickname "pepperwood" because when the thick, dark green leaves are crushed, they give off a scent like pepper. It's native to coastal forests and the Sierra foothills of California. It's a **Lauraceae** (laurel) family member and is commonly called the Oregon myrtle.

Locate: Bay Laurels occur in oak woodland near the coast and northern California, where moisture is sufficient, usually in or near riparian areas.

Identification:

GROWTH/SIZE - Depending on growing conditions, it can grow up to 40-80 feet tall and 30-60 feet wide.

BARK/STEM/ROOT - The bark is smooth and greenish-gray when young, becoming darker and rougher with age. The stems are thick and sturdy, with a reddish-brown color. The tree's roots can extend deep into the soil, making it well-adapted to drought conditions.

LEAF - The leaves are glossy and leathery, with a lance or oblong shape that tapers at both ends. They are dark green on the upper surface and paler green on the lower surface and can measure 4-10 inches long and 1-3 inches wide.

FLOWER - The flowers are small, yellow-green, and fragrant. They are in clusters on long stalks and bloom in late winter or early spring. Each flower measures up to 1/4 inch in diameter.

FRUIT/SEED/NUT - The fruit is a small, round, green berry that turns black when mature; it ripens from September to November. Each berry is about 1/2 inch in diameter and contains a single seed. The seed has a hard, woody shell and is edible but not commonly consumed.

Look-a-like(s): *Pacific wax myrtle* (*Myrica californica*) has similar glossy, leathery leaves but narrower and longer. The bark is gray-brown and scaly. *True bay laurel* (*Laurus nobilis*) has similar lance-shaped leaves but is smaller and more delicate. The bark is smooth and light brown.

Caution: Contact with the leaves, bark, or fruit of the tree can cause skin irritation in some people, similar to poison oak or poison ivy. It is advisable to wear protective gloves and clothing when handling the tree.

Culinary preparation: The fruit of the tree is edible, but it is not widely consumed. The berries have a strong and spicy flavor similar to allspice. The leaves can be used fresh or dried and are highly aromatic. The oil extracted from the tree's nuts is highly valued for its taste and aroma. It is often used in producing soaps, perfumes, and candles and in culinary applications like salad dressings and marinades.

Medicinal properties: Native American tribes' traditional medicinal uses include treating respiratory ailments and digestive issues. The leaves and bark were used topically to treat headaches. Modern medicinal uses need to be better established, but studies show several benefits for this plant. It's been found to have antimicrobial, antioxidant, and anti-inflammatory activity. It may have anti-cancer activity as well.

Fun Fact: It is considered an excellent tonewood sought by luthiers and woodworkers.

Dog Toxicity: This one is safe for your pup; however, large portions are likely to cause digestive issues such as vomiting and diarrhea. One widespread use for the leaves is to put them between the bed mattresses to eliminate or prevent flea infestations.

California Mountain Ash

Sorbus aucuparia [SOR-bus awk-yoo-PAR-ee-uh]

The name "rowan" comes from the Old Norse word "raun," which means "red," about the bright red berries that the tree produces. It's a **Rosaceae** (rose) family member; common names include Rowan, European mountain ash, and quickbeam.

Locate: Rowan grows not only in forests but also in parks, gardens, and along streets: woods, borders of swamps, and rocky hillsides at higher elevations.

Identification:

GROWTH/SIZE - a small to a medium-sized deciduous tree that can grow up to 50 feet in height and spread up to 30 feet.

BARK/STEM/ROOT - Its bark is smooth and gray-brown when young but develops shallow fissures and scaly plates as it ages. The stem is straight and slender, and the roots are shallow and fibrous.

LEAF - The leaves are pinnate, with 5-9 leaflets elliptical to ovate, measuring 2-4 inches long.

FLOWER - In late spring to early summer, it produces clusters of small, white, or pinkish flowers that measure around 3-5 inches in diameter.

FRUIT/SEED/NUT - The flowers are followed by bright red or orange-red round or pear-shaped berries measuring 1/2 inch in diameter. The seeds are tiny and brown and are contained within the fleshy fruit.

Look-a-like(s): *Common hawthorn* (*Crataegus monogyna*) leaves resemble Rowan but are more deeply lobed. *European bird cherry* (*Prunus padus*) leaves are similar to Rowan leaves but have a more pointed tip.

Caution: The thorns on the branches can be sharp and may cause injury, so it's essential to use caution when handling the tree. The seeds and leaves contain low levels of cyanogenic glycosides, which can release cyanide when consumed in large quantities. While the risk of poisoning from eating the berries is low, it's best to avoid consuming them in large amounts.

Culinary preparation: The high pectin content in the berries makes them ideal for making jams and jellies. The tart flavor of the berries pairs well with other fruits, like apples and pears. It can be used to make sauces, syrups, cakes, muffins and fermented to make a traditional European beverage called Rowanberry wine.

Medicinal properties: Traditional medicinal uses include treating digestive issues, respiratory infections, skin conditions, and menstrual cramps. Modern studies show the fruit contains high levels of antioxidants and may have the potential as a natural treatment for diabetes. The leaves and bark contain compounds that have anti-inflammatory and pain-relieving properties.

Fun Fact: In Norse mythology, a Rowan tree saved the life of Thor by bending over a fast-flowing river in the Underworld, where he was being swept away. Thor managed to grab the tree and get back to the shore. In Scandinavia, a rowan growing in a rock crevice or cleft held even greater magic. These trees were known as 'flying rowans.' To perform divination, the runes were inscribed on the rowan wood.

Pet Toxicity: Rowan berries are dangerous because they contain toxins. They can cause vomiting, diarrhea, and excessive salivation.

Common Fig
Ficus carica [FY-kus KA-ri-ka]

The fig was one of the earliest fruit trees to be cultivated, and its cultivation spread in remote ages over all the districts around the Aegean Sea and throughout the Levant. It is a species of small tree in the **Moraceae** (Mulberry) family, and the other name is the Edible fig.

Locate: It can be found among rocks, in woods, and scrub on hot, dry soils.

Identification:

GROWTH/SIZE - The size can vary depending on the growing conditions and pruning. It can reach a height of 10-30 feet and a spread of 10-30 feet.

BARK/STEM/ROOT - The bark is smooth and grey, and the stem can grow up to 12 inches in diameter. The roots are shallow and can spread out over a wide area.

LEAF - The leaves are large and lobed, with a length of 3-10 inches and a width of 2-6 inches. They are green and glossy on the top and lighter green on the bottom.

FLOWER - The flowers are small, 1/4 to 1/2 inch long. They are enclosed within a hollow receptacle called a syconium, which eventually develops into the fruit.

FRUIT/SEED/NUT - The fruit is an inverted inflorescence (syconium) with the flowers and seeds enclosed within a fleshy receptacle. The syconium can vary in size and shape, from round to oblong, and can grow up to 2-5 inches. When ripe, the fruit's skin is thin and can be green, yellow, purple, or black. The flesh of the fruit is sweet and can contain many tiny seeds.

Look-a-like(s): *Chinese banyan* (*Ficus microcarpa*) is often mistaken for the Fig. It is a tree or shrub that can grow up to 50 feet tall, with small, glossy leaves similar to Fig. *White mulberry* (*Morus alba*) has lobed leaves similar in shape to Fig, and the fruit is a cluster of small, juicy berries not enclosed within a fleshy receptacle.

Caution: The green parts' milky sap is irritating to human skin. The sap can be a severe eye irritant.

Culinary preparation: Fresh figs are in season from August to early October. They should be plump, soft, and without bruising or splits when used in cooking. If they smell sour, the figs have become over-ripe. Figs can be eaten fresh, dried, or processed into jam, rolls, biscuits, and other types of desserts. Slightly under-ripe figs can be kept at room temperature for 1–2 days to ripen before serving. Figs are most flavorful at room temperature.

Medicinal properties: In traditional medicine, the common fig has long existed. They contain a high amount of fiber and act as natural laxatives. A poultice made from the leaves promotes wound healing, relieves inflammation, and treats respiratory problems. Modern medicinal studies have shown they can lower blood sugar levels and protect the cardiovascular system. Antioxidants and anti-inflammatory compounds are abundant in figs. Researchers have found that Ficus carica compounds may have anti-cancer properties, potentially useful in cancer prevention.

Fun Fact: The fig and the fig tree were closely linked with female sexuality. This may account for the everyday use of the fig tree as a symbol of man's enlightenment, which was formerly supposed to come through his connection with the female principle.

Dog Toxicity: This one is tough. The fruit is good for your pup's digestive system, but the fig plant contains a toxic, sap-like substance known as ficin, which is toxic when consumed or when it comes into contact with the skin, eyes, or mouth of dogs.

D esert Ironwood

Olneya tesota [OL-NAY-UH TEH-SO-TUH]

Ironwoods are "nurse" trees in the Sonoran Desert. Animals gather in the shade during the hottest months. It's a member of the **Fabaceae** (legume) family.

Locate: Foothill washes and low desert areas in the Sonoran Desert

Identification:

GROWTH/SIZE - this is a slow-growing tree native to the Sonoran Desert. It is a small to medium-sized tree that can reach a height of 25-30 feet and a spread of 20-25 feet.

BARK/STEM/ROOT - The tree has a thick, gnarled, and twisted trunk of 1-2 feet in diameter. The bark is dark brown, rough, and fissured, protecting against fire, grazing, and other disturbances.

LEAF - The leaves are small, oval-shaped, and compound, measuring 1-2 inches long and 1 inch wide. They are arranged alternately on the stem and have a bright green color. The leaves are shed during the dry season to conserve water and reduce the risk of desiccation.

FLOWER - The flowers are showy and fragrant, with a sweet, vanilla-like scent. They are arranged in dense clusters or spikes, measuring 1-2 inches long and 1 inch wide. The flowers are bisexual and have five petals, which are white or pinkish-purple. The flowers bloom in the spring or summer, depending on the location and climate.

FRUIT/SEED/NUT - The fruit is a large, woody pod measuring 4-8 inches long and 1-2 inches wide. The pod contains several large, flat, black seeds measuring 1-2 inches long and 1 inch wide.

Look-a-like(s): *Blue Palo Verde (Parkinsonia florida)* and the *Catclaw Acacia (Acacia constricta)* have similar light red/brownish seedpods. Catclaw acacia seedpods are shorter and J-shaped.

Caution: The thorns on Ironwood can be sharp and painful if stepped on or brushed against.

Culinary preparation: The flowers bloom in late April-May, and seed pods in June-July. Ironwood flowers can be eaten raw in salads or candied for use in desserts. They are highly nutritious and rich in protein, fiber, and healthy fats. The seeds have a mild, nutty flavor and can be eaten raw or roasted in a pan or oven. They can also be ground into flour for baking, as a thickener for soups and stews, or into a paste mixed with honey or agave nectar to make a spreadable "Ironwood butter" and used as a condiment or added to smoothies, oatmeal, or other dishes. Soak the seeds in oil to infuse their flavor and nutrients and use it as a salad dressing or cooking oil.

Medicinal properties: Traditional medicinal properties of Ironwood include anti-inflammatory for pain and swelling, digestive aid for indigestion and stomach cramps, a natural antiseptic for wounds or burns, respiratory conditions such as asthma and bronchitis, and a blood cleanser to promote overall health. Modern preliminary studies show it's a rich source of antioxidants and antimicrobial properties helpful in fighting bacterial and fungal infections. Anti-cancer properties, the tree's bark has potent cytotoxic activity against several cancer cell lines, and cardiovascular properties show an ability to lower blood pressure.

Fun Fact: Desert Ironwood is perhaps one of the most highly regarded woods in knife-making. Its density, stability, grain patterns, and colors create a unique combination of characteristics ideal for decorative handles.

Dog Toxicity: no known toxicity

Western Redbud

Cercis occidentalis [SUR-sis ock-si-den-TAY-lis]

Because of their popularity as landscape plants, you will likely spot redbuds along sidewalks, public land, and parks. This beautiful tree is native to California and is a member of the **Fabaceae** (legume) family. It is also known as a California Redbud.

Locate: It is located in the foothills and mountains of California. It often grows on dry slopes in the mountain foothills in its range's northern, rainier parts. In its southern and drier range, it often grows near high-elevation creeks, canyon bottoms, and other moist environments.

Identification:

GROWTH/SIZE - a deciduous tree that typically grows to 10-30 feet and has a spread of 10-20 feet. It has a round, spreading shape and a moderately fast growth rate.

BARK/STEM/ROOT - The bark is smooth and grayish-brown. The stems and roots are also smooth and have a similar color to the bark. The shallow roots can spread widely, making the tree well-suited to rocky or shallow soil.

LEAF - The leaves are heart-shaped and measure 2-6 inches in length and width. They are a medium green color and have a slightly glossy appearance. The leaves emerge in the spring and turn yellow or orange in the fall.

FLOWER - the flower is one of its most striking features. They are bright pink or magenta and appear in clusters on the branches in the spring. The flowers are pea-shaped and measure about 1 inch in length.

FRUIT/SEED/NUT has a flat, brown seed pod 2-4 inches long. The pod is initially green and turns brown as it matures. The seeds are small and brown and are dispersed by wind or animals.

Look-a-like: none known

Caution: none known

Prepare: Edible flowers have a mild, nutty flavor. Its tiny pink to purple flowers can be easily identified from March to May. Before opening, the flower buds are usually deep pink and shaped like tulips. They are most flavorful when they first open. You can pickle them, use them as a garnish, or add them to salads. The seed pods are brown, flat, and slightly sweet and tangy. They can be eaten raw or cooked and served as a spice or seasoning. They can also be baked, ground into flour, or used in soups and stews as thickeners. You can also eat young leaves raw or cooked.

Medicinal Properties: Some Native American tribes traditionally used them for their medicinal properties. A decoction made from the bark is said to have a soothing effect on the lungs and airways. Tea made from leaves is said to have a calming effect on the digestive system. A poultice of the bark was applied to the affected area to prevent infection and promote healing. The bark and leaves have been used to treat menstrual problems. Though only a little has been done, modern preliminary studies have shown it is a rich source of antioxidants. It contains flavonoids, which can reduce inflammation in the body and may have the potential as a natural remedy for hypertension.

Fun Fact: In some Native American cultures, the Western Redbud symbolized renewal and rebirth. The tree was believed to have the power to bring new life and energy to those feeling stagnant or stuck.

Pet Toxicity: Though not known to be toxic, the tree's seed pods can be messy when they fall and may attract insects or rodents to the area, creating a risk of secondary toxicity if a dog ingests these animals.

PART SIX
BEYOND THE BUTTON
DISCOVERING THE DIVERSITY OF EDIBLE MUSHROOMS AND FUNGI IN CALIFORNIA

The experience of mushroom foraging can be rewarding and fun. However, it is essential to correctly identify mushrooms before consuming them. Learning how to identify mushrooms by using field guides, taking foraging classes, or observing experienced foragers is critical. You should pay close attention to the cap, stem, and gills' shape, color, and texture. It is also crucial to consider the mushroom's habitat and the plants and trees it grows near.

Many poisonous mushrooms can cause severe illness or even death if ingested. Whenever you are foraging, stay away from mushrooms with white gills. Additionally, many poisonous mushrooms have red pigmentation on their caps or stem.

Whenever possible, be cautious and only consume mushrooms that an expert has positively identified. It would be best never to eat raw mushrooms because some toxic mushrooms can cause severe reactions. It is also important to remember that even though the mushroom is edible, some people will still experience allergic reactions. Therefore, starting small is essential when trying a new mushroom species.

It is generally recommended that dogs not be allowed to eat wild mushrooms, as it can be challenging to identify toxic species, and even a tiny amount of a poisonous mushroom can be harmful to a dog. It is best to err on the side of caution and keep your dog away from wild mushrooms.

A m
methyst Deceiver
Laccaria amethystina [LUH-KAR-ee-uh AM-UH-THIS-tin-UH]

This mushroom is called the "deceiver" because its color can change depending on the humidity and the lighting conditions, making it challenging to identify. It is a member of the **Hydnangiaceae** family and is known by other names such as Lilac Laccaria and Purple-gilled Laccaria.

Locate: It is abundant under beech trees among all types of woodland leaf litter.

Identification:

GROWTH/SIZE - It typically grows 2-4 inches tall.

CAP - The cap is convex when young and becomes flattened with age, measuring 1-2 inches in diameter. The color of the cap varies from pale lilac to deep purple.

HYMENIUM - is located on the underside of the cap and has closely spaced gills. The gills measure about 1-2 mm in width.

STIPE - is slender and measures about 2-3 inches long and 1-2 mm wide. The color of the stipe is usually the same as the cap or slightly lighter.

SPORE PRINT - The spore print is white. The shape of the spores is elliptical and measures about 7-10 μm in length.

SMELL/TASTE - has a slightly nutty flavor and no discernible smell.

Look-a-like(s): *Lilac fibrecap* (*Inocybe geophylla lilacina*) is a possible look-alike. A Lilac fibrecap is distinguished by its gills. Its gills are off-white to gray, whereas the amethyst deceivers are the same color as its cap and stem.

Caution: The Amethyst deceiver itself is not toxic. However, metal can accumulate in areas polluted with arsenic and reach toxic levels within the mushroom flesh.

Culinary Preparation: The mushroom has a mild flavor and a tender texture, making it a versatile ingredient in many dishes. It is essential to cook it properly before consuming it. It can be sautéed or stir-fried with garlic, butter, and other seasonings and used as a side dish or topping for meats and vegetables. It can be added to soups and stews to add flavor and nutrition. It can be used as a topping for pasta dishes, cooked with pasta and sauce for added flavor, or in a creamy risotto alone or with other mushrooms. Lastly, it can be added to omelets and frittatas for a flavorful and nutritious breakfast or brunch dish.

Medicinal Properties: Some Native American cultures believe it has anti-inflammatory and analgesic properties. Some of the reported modern medicinal uses are anti-inflammatory, which may make it beneficial for reducing inflammation in the body—antioxidants, which can help to protect the body against free radical damage. Immune system support may make it helpful in preventing or treating infections and anti-cancer, which may have anti-cancer properties, although more research is needed to confirm these findings.

Fun Fact: In Scotland, stepping on a Laccaria amethystina mushroom is believed to cause the toes to turn to stone. In other cultures, the mushroom is associated with magical properties and is considered a good luck charm.

Black Morel

Morchella angusticeps [MORE-KEH-LUH AN-GUS-TY-SEPS]

Morels are known for their unique and intricate appearance, with a honeycomb-like structure that makes them instantly recognizable. They belong to the **Morchellaceae** family and are commonly called Thin-footed morel, Narrow-head morel, Small morel, Pointed morel, and Slender morel.

Locate: They can be found in various habitats, such as forests, fields, and gardens.

Identification:

CAP - shaped like a cone or a honeycomb, with a diameter of up to 2 inches. The color can range from light yellow to brown and is covered with deep pits and ridges.

HYMENIUM - located on the ridges and pits of the cap. The ridges are lined with numerous tiny, closely packed, vertical ridges, forming a honeycomb-like structure.

STIPE - typically light-colored, from white to yellow or light brown. It is cylindrical and can reach 3 inches tall.

SPORE PRINT - is white or cream-colored, and the spores are elliptical or spindle-shaped, measuring 18-23 by 10-14 microns.

TASTE / SMELL - has a delicate, nutty flavor that chefs and gourmets highly prize. Its aroma is subtle, with notes of earth and forest.

Look-a-like: *False morels* (*Gyromitra species*) [`toxic`] have a brain-like or wrinkled cap surface attached to the stem rather than entirely separate. *Wrinkled Thimble Cap* (*Verpa bohemica*) [`edible`] has a morel-like shape, but its cap is more elongated and has a smoother surface.

Caution: When harvesting morels, keep the base intact by cutting them at ground level with a sharp knife or scissors. Pulling the mushroom out of the ground can damage the mycelium, making it difficult for morels to grow in the future.

Culinary Preparation: Morels can be challenging to clean, as small bugs and debris are often trapped in their ridges and pits. Avoid soaking them in water, as this can cause them to become waterlogged and lose flavor. When cooking with them, they can be sautéed in butter or olive oil and used as a flavorful addition to many dishes, such as omelets, pasta dishes, risottos, and grilled sauces or roasted, which enhances their smoky, earthy flavor. They can be used as a side dish or added to salads and sandwiches, dried and rehydrated for later use, and are a great addition to soups and stocks, adding depth and complexity to the taste. They can also be a beautiful and tasty garnish for many dishes, such as roasted meats or vegetables.

Medicinal Properties: Though the morel is primarily valued for its culinary uses, some cultures have traditionally used morels for their potential therapeutic properties. Morels are a source of beta-glucans, a polysaccharide shown to support the immune system, and have been shown to have anti-tumor properties.

Fun Fact: During the reign of King Louis XIV of France, morels were considered a delicacy and were highly prized by the royal court. Legend has it that the king enjoyed morels so much that he ordered his gardeners to cultivate them, but they were unsuccessful in their attempts. The king then offered a large reward to anyone who could successfully cultivate morels. The challenge was finally taken up by a peasant farmer who claimed to have discovered the secret of growing morels. The farmer was summoned to the palace to share his secret with the king, but when he arrived, he was found to have already sown the spores in his field, and the morels had already begun to grow.

Cauliflower

Sparassis crispa [SPUH-RAS-iss KRIS-puh]

This mushroom is highly prized in Japanese and Korean cuisine and used in soups, stews, and stir-fry dishes. It's a member of the **Sparassidaceae** family and is commonly called Brain mushroom and Shrimp mushroom.

Locate: it grows in clusters or tufts on the ground, typically in forests and woodlands.

Identification:

GROWTH / SIZE - It can reach up to 20 inches tall and 12 inches wide, with an irregularly shaped cap that resembles a large, convoluted brain.

CAP - The cap color is pale to dark brown, with a rough, wrinkled surface.

HYMENIUM - is smooth and cream-colored and forms gill-like structures up to 1 inch long.

STIPE - is thick, curved, and often fused to other stems, and it can range from 2 to 8 inches long and up to 2 inches wide. The stipe color is similar to the cap, with a rough and scaly texture.

SPORE PRINT - The spore print is white or cream-colored.

SMELL / TASTE - has a sweet, nutty flavor and a slightly crunchy texture when cooked.

Look-a-like: *Clustered coral* (*Ramaria botrytis*) [edible] has a branching, coral-like fruiting body ranging from pinkish-orange to yellowish-brown. *Hen of the woods* (*Grifola frondosa*) [edible] has a more complex structure with multiple branching stems and clusters of overlapping, fan-shaped caps and is generally brownish-gray.

Caution: Wild mushrooms can absorb toxins and pollutants from their environment, so it's essential to be sure that the mushrooms are harvested from a safe location. Avoid collecting mushrooms from areas that may have been exposed to pollution or toxins, such as near roads, factories, or agricultural fields.

Culinary Preparation: It's a popular ingredient in many cuisines. It should be thoroughly cooked before consumption to avoid any potential digestive upset. Some may find the texture of the mushroom to be somewhat tough or fibrous, so it's essential to cook it properly to ensure it's tender and palatable. It can be sautéed with garlic, herbs, butter, or oil for a simple and delicious side dish. It's ideal for stir-frying with vegetables and meat for a flavorful and nutritious dish. It can be added to soups, stews, and other savory dishes to add depth and richness to the flavor. It can be dried and rehydrated later for use in various recipes. It has a concentrated flavor that can be added to soups, stews, and other dishes for a rich, umami taste.

Medicinal Properties: While more research is needed to fully understand its medicinal properties, some potential health benefits include polysaccharides, which have been shown to enhance immune system function and improve infection resistance. Some studies have suggested that it may have anti-inflammatory properties, making it helpful in treating certain inflammatory conditions, such as rheumatoid arthritis. It may help lower cholesterol levels in the blood, making it a beneficial ingredient in managing cardiovascular health.

Fun Fact: In many countries, including Japan and Korea, Sparassis crispa is a popular mushroom for hunting and gathering. In Japan, it's known as "hanetake" or "fire mushroom" because of the bright orange color that the mushroom can take on when cooked.

Crab Brittle Gill
Russula xerampelina [RUH-SOO-luh zeh-ram-PEL-in-uh]

This mushroom is also known to form mycorrhizal associations with various tree species, which helps to facilitate the exchange of nutrients between the tree roots and the surrounding soil. It's a member of the **Russulaceae** family and is often called Shrimp Russula and Shrimpy Brittlegill.

Locate: This popular edible mushroom can be found in deciduous and coniferous forests throughout California.

Identification:

GROWTH/SIZE - it can grow to 4 inches tall and 4 inches wide.

CAP - it has a convex cap about 1-3 inches in diameter, with a central depression. The color of the cap ranges from violet-gray to dark brown, with a slightly rough or velvety texture.

HYMENIUM - it's made up of gills that are adnate or slightly decurrent. They are about 1-2 inches long and white, eventually turning cream-colored with age. The mushroom's gills are white and brittle, hence the common name "Brittlegill."

STIPE - is cylindrical and measures about 1-2 inches long and 1 inch in diameter. It is white and sometimes turns a faint pinkish color towards the base.

SPORE PRINT - is cream-colored, and the spores are elliptical and measure about 7-9 x 6-7 micrometers.

SMELL / TASTE - it's known for its distinctive seafood-like aroma and taste.

Look-a-like(s): *The Sickener* (*Russula emetica*) [toxic] cap is typically bright red with a smooth and shiny surface. The gills are white and close together, and the stem is white or pale. It's generally found in coniferous forests, often associated with spruce or fir trees.

Caution: Some may experience digestive upset or other gastrointestinal symptoms after consuming, mainly if cooked incorrectly.

Culinary Preparation: It is a delicious and versatile mushroom that can be used in various culinary applications. As with all mushrooms, it can be added to stir-fries, soups, and the like. Due to its slightly nutty, seafood-like flavor, it pairs well with various herbs and seasonings, so it can be sautéed for a delicious side dish or grilled or roasted to bring out its nutty, slightly smoky flavor.

Medicinal Properties: Primarily valued for its culinary uses, it has shown positive effects during limited research and has been shown to have anti-tumor and anti para-sitic activity.

Fun Fact: The mushroom's cap contains a red pigment that can be extracted and used to dye fabrics a deep, rich shade of red. Traditional craftspeople and weavers once used the pigment to create beautiful, long-lasting textiles.

H edgehog
hydnum repandum [HYE-DNUM REH-PAN-DUM]

The Hedgehog mushroom got its name from its spiky appearance, resembling a hedgehog's quills. Commonly known as the sweet tooth or pied de mouton, it is a fungus that belongs to the **Hydnaceae** family.

Locate: It is found in North America, Europe, and Asia and grows in deciduous and coniferous forests, especially in late summer and fall.

Identification:

CAP - The cap is round or slightly flattened, with a diameter ranging from 2 to 8 inches. It is covered with spines, usually 1/2 to 1 inch long, instead of gills. The cap color can vary from creamy white to yellowish-brown or reddish-brown.

HYMENIUM - The hymenium is irregularly shaped and can be found on the underside of the cap. It is usually cream to pale yellow and can measure up to 1 inch in thickness.

STIPE - The stipe is relatively short, 1 to 3 inches long, and 1/2 to 1 inch in diameter. It is usually white to pale yellow and has a smooth or slightly velvety surface.

SPORE PRINT - The spore print is white, and the spores are ellipsoid or subglobose in shape, measuring 4-6 x 3-5 μm.

SMELL / TASTE - has a mild, nutty flavor and a slightly sweet aroma.

Look-a-like: *Depressed Hedgehog* (*Hydnum umbilicatum*) [edible] grows in swamps and bogs but is smaller and has a darker cap.

Caution: none known as look-a-likes are edible.

Culinary Preparation: This mushroom is a popular edible in Europe and North America, often used in soups, stews, and risotto. It's known for absorbing and retaining flavors, making it a popular ingredient in savory dishes.

Medicinal Properties: has been used to treat various ailments, including arthritis, gout, and stomach problems. Its also thought to have anti-inflammatory and anti-tumor effects.

Fun Fact: In some cultures, the Hedgehog mushroom is believed to have mystical or magical properties and is used in spiritual ceremonies and rituals.

Oak Chanterelle
Cantharellus californicus [KAN-THUH-REL-UHS KUH-LUH-FOR-NI-KUHSS]

It is a species of edible mushroom that is native to California. It belongs to the **Cantharellaceae** family and is often called California chanterelle or Golden chanterelle.

Locate: a mycorrhizal mushroom that grows in coniferous and mixed forests such as Douglas fir and oak. It typically appears in late summer and early fall.

Identification:

CAP - The cap can range from 1 to 5 inches in diameter, and the entire mushroom can grow up to 6 inches tall. It's vase-shaped, with a wavy, irregular margin, usually bright yellow to orange-yellow, but can also be reddish or brownish in some specimens. The surface is smooth and slightly moist.

HYMENIUM - The hymenium is composed of shallow ridges instead of traditional gills. These ridges are forked and run down the length of the stipe. They are usually lighter than the cap, ranging from pale yellow to cream.

STIPE - The stipe is thick and fleshy and may be either solid or hollow. It is usually the same color as the cap or slightly lighter. The stipe can grow up to 3 inches long and 1 inch wide.

Sᴘᴏʀᴇ ᴘʀɪɴᴛ - The spore print is white to pale yellow. The spores themselves are elliptical and measure around 8-10 micrometers long.

Sᴍᴇʟʟ/Tᴀsᴛᴇ - a sweet, fruity odor sometimes described as apricot-like. Its taste is rich and savory, with a slightly nutty flavor. It is considered to be one of the best-tasting of all wild mushrooms.

Look-a-like: *Jack O'Lantern Mushroom* (*Omphalotus olearius*) [toxic] is similar but has a gilled underside instead of ridges. It also has distinctive bioluminescence, which means it glows in the dark. *False Chanterelle* (*Hygrophoropsis aurantiaca*) [toxic] has a similar shape and color but a smoother cap and gills underneath instead of ridges. It also has a slightly different scent.

Caution: Oak Chanterelles, like most mushrooms, are best consumed as fresh as possible. If you must store them, do so in a paper bag in the refrigerator, and use them within a few days.

Culinary Preparation: The Oak chanterelle is a popular and flavorful wild mushroom. One of the most common ways to prepare Oak Chanterelles is to sauté them. The meaty texture of the mushrooms pairs well with the rich, savory flavors of these ingredients. After being sautéed, they can be added to soups, salads, pasta sauce, or anything. Add the mushrooms to any basic risotto recipe, along with Parmesan cheese and fresh herbs, for a comforting and delicious meal. Throw them on skewers or a grill basket for a smoky, charred flavor. Before grilling, brush the mushrooms with olive oil and season with salt and pepper.

Medicinal Properties: In traditional Chinese medicine, Chanterelles have been used to treat various ailments, including high blood pressure and digestive problems. The medicinal properties of Chanterelle mushrooms are still being studied today, and they are an important subject of research in the field of natural medicine.

Fun Fact: In Europe, Chanterelles have been prized for their culinary qualities since at least the 16th century, and they were considered a delicacy by the aristocracy.

Orange Peel
Aleuria aurantia [UH-LOOR-ee-uh aw-RAN-tee-uh]

The scientific name of *Aleuria aurantia* comes from the Greek word *aleuron*, which means flour and refers to the powdery texture of the fruiting bodies. It's part of the **Pyronemataceae** family and has other common names, such as Orange Peel Fungus and Orange Cup Fungus.

Locate: appears in the fall or winter, commonly found in clusters or scattered in grassy areas, such as lawns, meadows, or forest clearings. It prefers well-drained, nutrient-poor soils and is often associated with mosses and lichens.

Identification:

CAP - its size ranges from 1-4 inches in diameter and is typically orange to reddish-orange. The cap is shaped like a shallow bowl or cup, with a smooth and slightly wrinkled surface texture.

HYMENIUM - located on the underside of the cap and consists of densely packed, radiating gills. The gills are about 1/2 inch long and are typically the same color as the cap.

STIPE - usually absent or short, less than 1/4 inch long, and the same color as the cap. The mushroom has a mycelial attachment point that anchors it to the substrate.

Spore print - produces a white to pale-yellow spore print, with spores measuring about 7-10 micrometers in diameter.

Look-a-like: *Sowerbyella rhenana* has a stipe and is smaller than its cousin.

Caution: Like many other types of fungi, the orange peel fungus releases spores into the air. While these spores are not generally harmful to humans, individuals with respiratory conditions like asthma may wish to avoid handling the fungus.

Culinary Preparation: With a delicious, deep smoky taste and a meaty texture, it is a delightful treat when fried in butter until it starts popping. Sadly, finding it in abundance has been a problem.

Medicinal Properties: has been used in traditional Chinese medicine for its anti-inflammatory properties though no research has been done on everyday uses.

Fun Fact: The fungus is saprobic, meaning it feeds on dead organic matter and helps to break it down into nutrients that other organisms can use. It's also sometimes used as a natural dye for textiles and paper, producing a yellow-orange color.

Pine Mushroom
Tricholoma magnivelare [TRIH-KOH-LOH-MUH MAG-NUH-VUH-LAIR-EE]

A highly prized and sought-after edible mushroom is known for its complex flavor and aroma. It belongs to the **Tricholomataceae** family and is commonly known as the "matsutake mushroom."

Locate: a mycorrhizal species found in the northern hemisphere, particularly in coniferous forests.

Identification:

CAP - usually 2-8 inches in diameter and has a convex to flat shape. The color of the cap varies from light beige to reddish-brown, with a rough, scaly surface.

HYMENIUM - made up of closely packed gills that are attached to the stipe. The gills are white to cream-colored and can be up to 1 inch long.

STIPE - usually 2-6 inches long and 1/2 - 1 inch thick. It is typically white to cream-colored and has a smooth, dry surface. The stipe often tapers towards the base and may have a small, cup-shaped volva at the bottom.

SPORE PRINT - White, and the spores themselves are ellipsoid and smooth. The size of the spores is about 7-10 micrometers long and 5-6 micrometers wide.

SMELL / TASTE - has a distinctive spicy and slightly piney odor, which is said to be similar to the smell of cinnamon or red hots. The taste of the mushroom is savory and umami, with a slightly sweet aftertaste.

Look-a-like: *False Matsutake* (*Sarcodon imbricatus*) is similar in appearance and is sometimes called the "scaly chanterelle" due to its scaly cap. However, the False Matsutake has gills under its cap, while the American Matsutake has pores. *Pine Mushrooms* (*Tricholoma magnificum and Tricholoma albobrunneum*) Pine mushrooms are another species of Tricholoma similar to the American Matsutake. They also have a distinctive aroma and are found in similar habitats. However, Pine Mushrooms tend to have a smoother cap.

Caution: none known

Culinary Preparation: The American Matsutake is highly valued for its aromatic flavor and meaty texture. It is used in various culinary preparations, especially in Japanese and other Asian cuisines. One of the most popular ways to prepare American Matsutake is to grill them with a bit of oil or butter and salt. The mushrooms' meaty texture and smoky flavor pair well with the grill's charred flavor. It's often used in soups and broths, such as the classic Japanese dish *Matsutake Dobinmushi*. It is a popular ingredient in sushi and can also be pickled alone or as part of a mixed vegetable pickle. The pickling process adds a tangy flavor to the mushrooms.

Medicinal Properties: American Matsutake contains beta-glucans, complex sugars shown to have immune-boosting properties. They are also rich in antioxidants, which may help to protect against cellular damage and reduce the risk of chronic diseases such as cancer.

Fun Fact: The American Matsutake has declined in some areas due to various factors, including habitat loss, climate change, and over-harvesting. This decline has raised concerns among those who rely on the mushroom for cultural, economic, and medicinal purposes.

Spring King Bolete (Porcini)

Boletus rex-veris [BOH-LEE-TUHS REKS-VER-IS]

A giant, edible mushroom that mushroom enthusiasts highly prize. It belongs to the **Boletaceae** family, which includes many other popular edible mushrooms such as porcini, chanterelles, and morel mushrooms.

Locate: This species grows in deciduous and mixed forests, often associated with oak, beech, and chestnut trees.

Identification:

GROWTH / SIZE - can grow up to 10 inches tall.

CAP - The cap is round or oval-shaped and can be up to 8 inches long. It is reddish-brown and covered with a fine layer of velvety fuzz. As the mushroom matures, the cap may crack and become more irregular.

HYMENIUM - The underside of the cap has a pore surface that contains the mushroom's reproductive structures, called tubes. The tubes are packed with tiny pores that release spores when the mushroom matures. The tubes can be up to 1 inch long.

STIPE - The stipe is thick and can be up to 4 inches long. It is reddish-brown and has a slightly rough texture. The stipe is also covered with a fine layer of fuzz, like the cap.

SPORE PRINT - The spore print is olive-brown and can be up to 2 inches in diameter.

Smell / Taste - It has a pleasant, nutty aroma and a rich, meaty flavor. It is considered one of the best-tasting wild mushrooms and is highly prized by gourmet cooks.

Look-a-like: *Porcini* (*Boletus edulis*) [edible] has a similar brown cap and a thick stem, but the cap is smoother and lacks the velvety fuzz present on Boletus rex-veris. *Slippery jack* (*Suillus luteus*) [edible] has a slimy cap and a sticky stem, distinguishing it from Boletus rex-veris.

Caution: Age and condition can affect its edibility. Too old, damaged, or contaminated mushrooms can be unsafe to eat.

Culinary Preparation: A highly sought-after wild mushroom that gourmet cooks prize for its delicious flavor and meaty texture. It can be sautéed in butter or olive oil and served as a side dish or added to pasta dishes, risottos, or omelets. It pairs well with other savory ingredients like garlic, shallots, and fresh herbs. It can also be grilled or roasted, which brings out its smoky, earthy flavors. It can be dried and used in soups, stews, or sauces throughout the year. Drying intensifies the taste of the mushroom, and it can be rehydrated for later use or preserved in oil, vinegar, or alcohol. This technique is especially popular in Italy, where they are used in antipasti dishes.

Medicinal Properties: While some claim this mushroom may have medicinal properties, limited scientific evidence supports these claims. It may have immune-boosting properties, anti-inflammatory properties, and antioxidant properties and may help to support digestive health and alleviate symptoms of gastrointestinal disorders.

Fun Fact: It has a long history of culinary use and was highly valued by the ancient Romans. The Roman poet Juvenal referred to boletus mushrooms as the "food of the gods."

PART SEVEN
THE OCEAN'S SUPERFOOD

EXPLORING THE NUTRITIONAL BENEFITS OF 5 SEAWEED TYPES

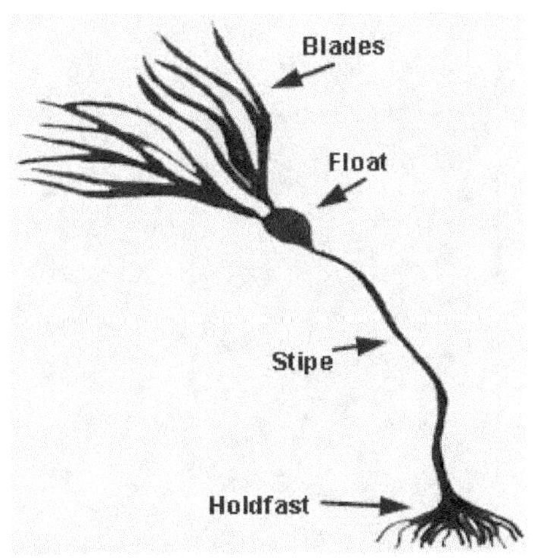

Bull Kelp

Nereocystis luetkeana [NAIR-EE-OH-SIS-TIS LOO-ET-KEE-AN-UH]

It belongs to the brown algae family, **Laminariaceae**. These seaweeds are important ecologically, providing habitat and food for various marine organisms.

Location: found in temperate and cold waters in rocky, intertidal, or sub-tidal areas, anchored to the ocean floor by a holdfast.

Identification:

GROWTH / SIZE: grows in long, cylindrical structures that can reach lengths of up to 100 feet, although the average size is typically between 20-60 feet.

BLADE: long and narrow, with a distinctive elongated oval shape that tapers to a point. It can grow up to 10 inches wide and 15-30 feet long, with a smooth, leathery texture. It's a dark olive-green color when young, but as it ages, it becomes brown and may have patches of lighter green.

FLOAT: a large, bulbous structure located at the top of the plant that can reach up to 10 inches in diameter and is responsible for keeping it upright in the water. The float is typically a deep golden brown color and has a smooth, waxy texture.

STIPE: The stipe is typically 1 inch in diameter, dark brown, and can be up to 90 feet long. The stipe is generally long and flexible, allowing the blade to move with the flow of the water.

Holdfast: is disc-shaped and can be up to 12 inches in diameter. It comprises a network of root-like structures that grip onto rocks and other surfaces, helping keep the kelp anchored in place. The color of the holdfast is also dark brown.

Look-alike(s): *Giant kelp* (*Macrocystis pyrifera*) is a type of kelp that can grow to over 100 feet long and is found in the same region. It has long, ribbon-like blades and floats on the water's surface in large, tangled mats.

Cautions: If you are collecting or harvesting bull kelp, be aware of the impact this may have on the ecosystem and consider sustainable harvesting practices.

Culinary Preparation: Bull kelp has a distinctive aroma often described as sweet and slightly smoky. It's often used to make a flavorful, nutrient-rich broth or stock and can be sliced thinly and added to salads and other side dishes for a nutritious and delicious addition. It can be pickled to create a tangy, crunchy snack or condiment. It can be substituted for nori or other seaweeds in sushi rolls, hand rolls, and other dishes, and it can be dried and ground into a powder.

Medicinal Properties: High fiber helps treat digestive disorders such as constipation and diarrhea. The seaweed's anti-inflammatory and antioxidant properties may help to soothe and heal irritated skin. It contains a wide range of vitamins, minerals, and antioxidants, which may help to boost the immune system and support overall health and well-being. It's a natural source of iodine. The antibacterial properties may help to prevent infection, while its high nutrient content may help to support the body's natural healing processes.

Fun Fact: Bull kelp was once used as a navigational aid by indigenous people in the Pacific Northwest. The long, flexible blades of the seaweed would point in the direction of the prevailing current, making it easier to navigate.

Dog Toxicity: Bull kelp contains a sugar molecule called alginate, which can cause gastrointestinal distress if consumed in large quantities. Symptoms include vomiting, diarrhea, and abdominal pain.

E elgrass
Zostera marina [ZOSS-ter-uh muh-REE-nuh]

Eelgrass is a crucial habitat for marine life, including sea turtles, crabs, and fish. It provides a safe place for them to lay eggs, seek shelter, and find food. Eelgrass species are also notable for their flowers, which lack petals. Instead, the flowers are enclosed within a sheath-like structure known as a spathe, which helps to protect them from damage in the harsh marine environment. It's a member of the **Zosteraceae** family of flowering plants that consists of marine and estuarine species.

Location: It grows in meadows on soft sediments and can tolerate various salinity and water clarity conditions.

Identification:

GROWTH / SIZE: It can grow up to 6 feet in length but typically ranges from 10 to 40 inches in height.

BLADE: long, narrow, and ribbon-like, with a pointed tip and a rounded base. The blade width can range from 1 to 6 millimeters. The color of the blades is a vibrant green and can appear glossy in the water.

FLOAT: has float-shaped leaves, which are called "floaters." These leaves are much wider than the blades and have a round or oval shape. The floaters are also green and can reach up to 6 inches long.

Stipe: typically around 1 to 2 millimeters thick and can grow up to 3 feet long. It is also green and can appear somewhat translucent.

Holdfast: is a complex network of rhizomes and roots that anchor the plant to the sediment. It can vary in size but typically measures around 1 to 2 inches in diameter. The shape of the holdfast is irregular, with numerous projections gripping the sediment.

Look-alike(s): *Scouler's surfgrass* (*Phyllospadix scouleri*) is a native plant that grows in the intertidal zone and looks similar to eelgrass. It has long, narrow leaves and produces small flowers on a spike. *Widgeon grass* (*Ruppia maritima*) is a seagrass that grows in shallow saltwater areas and has thin, ribbon-like leaves. It produces small, green flowers.

Cautions: Eelgrass is a crucial habitat for many marine species, so any disturbance or removal of eelgrass can negatively impact the local ecosystem. It's a protected species in many areas, so checking for any regulations or permits needed before harvesting or disturbing eelgrass beds is essential.

Culinary Preparation: The leaves and stems can be chopped and added to the dish for a mild, slightly salty flavor. The leaves can be washed and added to a salad mix for texture and flavor, wrapped around fish or seafood before cooking to add a subtle flavor, or steeped in hot water to make a mild, slightly salty tea.

Medicinal Uses: The leaves and stems can be boiled in water into tea to alleviate digestive discomfort or soothe respiratory issues such as coughs and colds. The leaves can be applied externally as a poultice to reduce inflammation and pain, and it has also been used as a diuretic to relieve water retention and promote urination.

Fun Fact: In the early 1900s, eelgrass was used as a filling material for some mattresses in the United States. Eelgrass was considered a comfortable and durable material for mattresses, but its use declined as synthetic materials became more widely available.

Dog Toxicity: Eelgrass is not considered toxic to dogs. If a dog ingests eelgrass accidentally, it is unlikely to cause significant health problems. However, dogs can experience mild digestive upset, such as vomiting or diarrhea, if they consume a large amount of eelgrass.

L ittle Rockweed
Fucus vesiculosus [FYOO-KUS VUH-SIK-YUH-LOH-SUS]

The **Fucaceae** family is a group of brown algae commonly referred to as "rockweeds" or "wracks." It provides habitat and food for many species of invertebrates and fish. Its physical characteristics allow it to survive in the challenging conditions of the intertidal zone, where it is exposed to air and water and is also known as Bladderwrack.

Location: They are found in the intertidal zone, where they attach to rocks and other hard substrates.

Identification:

GROWTH/SIZE: can grow up to 35 inches long and up to 2 inches wide.

BLADE: are flat and narrow, with a linear shape. They can range in color from yellow-green to dark brown and can be up to 14 inches long.

FLOAT: has air-filled bladders, which give it buoyancy and allow it to float near the water's surface. The bladders are typically brown or green and round or oval and can range in size from 1/4-1/2 inch in diameter.

STIPE: is cylindrical, can be up to 1/4 inch in diameter, and is usually brown.

HOLDFAST: a branched structure that anchors the seaweed to rocks or other rigid substrates. It is usually brown or black and can be up to 1 inch in diameter.

Look-alike(s): *Toothed wrack* (*Fucus serratus*) is closely related and has a similar appearance, with a brownish-green color and distinctive "bladders" along the branches. However, it has a more finely-branched structure, and the bladders are more elongated and flattened.

Cautions: Bladderwrack is a natural iodine source. However, excessive iodine intake can be harmful, particularly for people with thyroid conditions.

Culinary Preparation: It's a common ingredient in fish and seafood broths and stocks, adding depth and umami to the flavor. It can be used in salads, either fresh or rehydrated. It can be pureed or chopped and added to sauces and condiments, such as marinades, dips, and spreads. It pairs particularly well with seafood dishes like fish, shellfish, and sushi, and it can be added to bread, crackers, and other baked goods for added nutrition and flavor. The seaweed can be chopped, added to the dough, or incorporated as a powder or extract.

Medicinal Properties: It's a natural source of iodine. It contains various vitamins and minerals that are beneficial for skin health, including vitamins A and C, iodine, and calcium, and its shown to have immune system-enhancing properties. It has been shown to have anti-inflammatory properties and is used in traditional medicine to help treat various digestive issues, such as constipation, indigestion, and gastritis.

Fun Fact: In the past, bladderwrack was used as a source of iodine to produce gunpowder. During the 19th century, when gunpowder production was at its height, bladderwrack was collected from the shores of Scotland and other areas to extract iodine, a key component of gunpowder. The seaweed was burned to create a "kelp ash," which was then leached to remove the iodine. This process, known as "kelping," was an important industry in many coastal areas.

Dog Toxicity: Excessive iodine intake can harm dogs, particularly those with pre-existing thyroid conditions. Some dogs may experience digestive upset or other gastrointestinal symptoms.

Nori

Pyropia tenera [PY-ROH-pee-uh teh-NAIR-uh]

Nori is a type of edible seaweed that belongs to the red algae family known as **Porphyra**. It provides habitat and food for many marine life species and is an important food source for humans in many cultures.

Location: commonly found in the intertidal zone of rocky shorelines and other hard substrates in the Pacific Ocean.

Identification:

GROWTH/SIZE: It can grow up to 12 inches long, and the width of the blades can range from 2 to 8 inches.

BLADE: thin and papery, with a wavy or crinkled appearance. The blades can range from bright green to reddish-brown, depending on the age of the plant.

FLOAT: does not have float-shaped leaves, as it is a type of seaweed attached directly to rocks or other substrates in the intertidal zone.

STIPE: is short, cylindrical, and often difficult to see because the plant is thin. The color of the stipe is usually the same as the blades, ranging from green to reddish-brown.

HOLDFAST: disc-shaped, with a diameter of up to 3/4 inch. It can range from light to dark brown and anchors the plant to rocks or other hard substrates in the intertidal zone.

Look-a-like(s): *Irish moss* (*Chondrus crispus*) has a darker, more brownish-red color and is often used as a thickening agent in food.

Cautions: Nori is a rich source of iodine. Too much iodine can cause thyroid dysfunction, particularly in people with pre-existing thyroid conditions. Nori also contains high levels of vitamin K, which can interact with blood-thinning medications like warfarin.

Culinary Preparation: This red alga is commonly used in sushi and other Japanese dishes. Nori is perhaps most well-known for its use in sushi rolls. It's often eaten as a snack, either in small sheets or seasoned and toasted strips. It can be chopped or torn into small pieces and added to salads for a flavorful and nutritious boost, or miso soup, ramen, and other Japanese soups for added umami flavor. It can be finely ground and used as a seasoning or be cut into decorative shapes and used as a garnish for dishes like fried rice, stir-fries, and noodle dishes.

Medicinal Properties: Nori is a rich source of various vitamins and minerals, including iodine, vitamin C, vitamin A, and iron. It contains antioxidants, anti-inflammatory properties, and fiber that may benefit gut health. Some studies suggest that Nori may benefit cardiovascular health and help support the immune system and protect against infections.

Fun Fact: Nori is a fascinating and essential part of Japanese culture and cuisine. It has been used in Japan for over 1,300 years. It's not seaweed: it's red algae that grows in shallow waters along rocky coastlines.

In ancient Japan, Nori was considered a luxury food only consumed by the wealthy. Nori became more widely available and affordable in the Edo period (1603-1868).

The Nori Matsuri, or Nori Festival, is held every year in the town of Tateyama, Japan, to celebrate the harvesting and production of Nori. The festival includes traditional Japanese music, dance, and food.

Dog Toxicity: Small amounts of Nori are not likely harmful to most dogs. Some things to consider when feeding Nori to dogs include it being high in iodine and sodium. Some dogs may be allergic to it, contributing to symptoms like itching, hives, vomiting, and difficulty breathing.

W akame
Undaria pinnatifida [UHN-DAH-REE-UH PIN-UH-TIF-IH-DUH]

Wakame belongs to the family **Alariaceae**, which is a family of brown seaweeds. This family includes many different genera and species of seaweeds, many of which are used for food and other purposes.

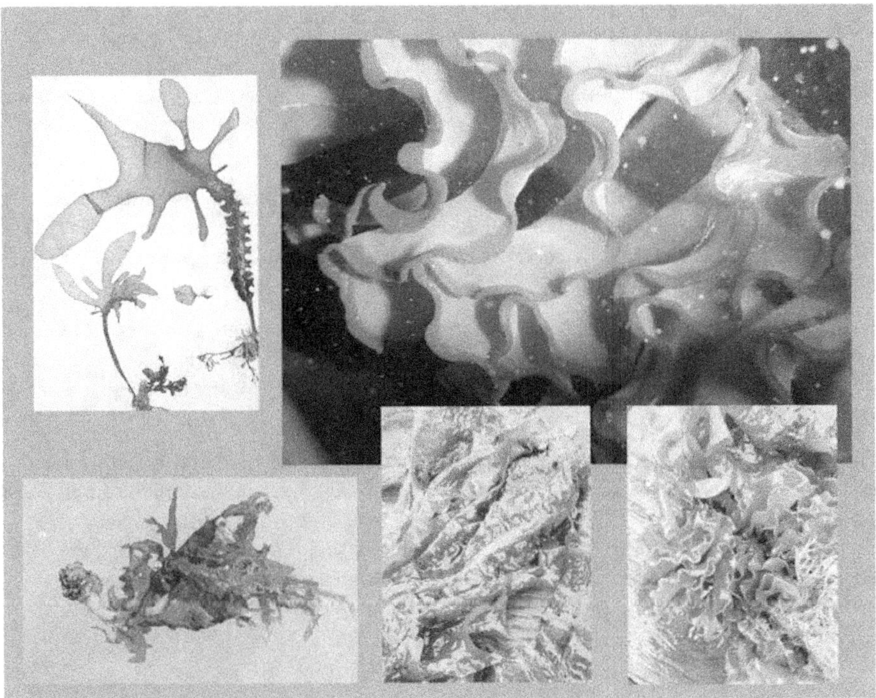

Location: particularly in areas with cold, nutrient-rich waters. It is most commonly found along the West Coast, from Alaska to California.

Identification:

GROWTH / SIZE: can grow to 4 feet long and 2 feet wide.

BLADE: The blade shape is long and ribbon-like, approximately 4 inches wide. Blade color can vary from greenish-brown to dark brown.

FLOAT: oval or elliptical, with a diameter of about 1/2 inch. The floats are usually located near the base of the blades and provide buoyancy for the plant.

STIPE: is cylindrical and can reach up to 1/4 inch in diameter. The stipe color is brownish-green or yellowish-brown.

HOLDFAST: a disk-like structure that attaches the plant to the substrate. The holdfast is usually brown and can range from 2 to 6 inches in diameter.

Look-alike(s): *Kombu* (*Saccharina japonica*) is a brown seaweed commonly used in Japanese cuisine. It resembles wakame, with long, flat fronds that can grow up to 4 meters long. *Oarweed* (*Laminaria digitata*) grows in cold, rocky coastal areas and has long, strap-like fronds that can grow up to 4 meters long. It has a slightly different appearance than wakame but is commonly used similarly in cuisine.

Cautions: Harvesting from the wild is regulated and requires a permit in many areas. In some cases, it may be illegal to harvest or possess the species. It is important to check local regulations before harvesting any wild seaweed.

Culinary Preparation: In areas where harvesting is allowed, it can be harvested by hand or with mechanical harvesters. Dehydrate it and then eat right off the rack. Alternatively, it can be chopped into rice, quinoa, soups, casseroles, stews, beans, and toast. You can always grind it in a coffee mill and sprinkle the flakes on salads, sandwiches, etc., as a salty addition.

Medicinal Properties: While primarily used as a food, Wakame has potential therapeutic uses. Some research has suggested that Wakame may have anti-inflammatory properties and is a good source of dietary fiber. It also contains compounds that may help to regulate blood sugar levels and is a rich source of iodine.

Fun Fact: In Japan, its sometimes used as an ingredient in cosmetics, as it is believed to have moisturizing and anti-aging properties. In some cultures, it is associated with good luck and prosperity. In Japan, it is often eaten at the beginning of the year as part of a traditional New Year's feast.

Dog Toxicity: Some evidence suggests that Wakame may be toxic to dogs in large quantities because it contains high levels of a sugar called fucoidan, which can be difficult for dogs to digest. If a dog consumes a small amount of Wakame, it is unlikely to cause any harm. However, if a dog ingests a lot of Wakame, it may experience symptoms such as vomiting, diarrhea, and abdominal pain. In severe cases, Wakame toxicity can lead to dehydration, electrolyte imbalances, and other serious health problems.

PART EIGHT
DEADLY BEAUTIES
IDENTIFYING AND UNDERSTANDING CALIFORNIA'S POISONOUS PLANTS

California Copperleaf

Acalypha californica [UH-KAL-uh-fuh kuh-luh-FOR-ni-kuh]

Acalypha californica is also known as Pringle's three-seeded mercury and California copperleaf. From the foothills of the Peninsular range down to the lower desert of San Diego County, it is the only Acalypha species native to California. This plant most commonly grows on crumbling granite rocks, ledges, and cliff faces, though it can occasionally be found in sand washes. It bears beautiful wavy hairy serrated leaves that are light green. It is common for younger leaves to have pink or red edges. Summer months bring pinkish or copper-colored leaves. The stems come in white, pink, or red colors. A bumpy pinkish-red spike, sometimes speckled with white, emerges from the base of each leaf stem.

Deadly Nightshade

atropa belladonna [AH-TROH-pah bel-lah-DON-nah]

Nightshade, a deadly nightshade or belladonna, is a highly toxic perennial plant. It can be found in some parts of North America where it has been introduced. Atropa belladonna is a nightshade family member, typically growing up to 6 feet tall. It has distinctive bell-shaped purple or green flowers, and its fruits are small green berries that turn black when ripe. The plant's leaves are large and dark green, emitting a foul odor when crushed. All parts of the plant, including the berries, leaves, and roots, contain toxic alkaloids such as atropine, hyoscyamine, and scopolamine, which can cause hallucinations, paralysis, and even death if ingested in large enough quantities. Despite its toxicity, atropa belladonna has been used for medicinal purposes. Still, its use is limited mainly to producing certain drugs under strict medical supervision.

Death Angel

Amanita ocreata [UH-MUH-NEE-tuh oh-KREE-uh-tuh]

Amanita ocreata, commonly known as the Western Destroying Angel or Death Angel, is a highly toxic mushroom in western North America. It is known for its lethal effects on humans and animals, causing severe liver and kidney damage, gastrointestinal symptoms, and potentially fatal consequences. It's identified by its white, smooth cap and stem, with a bulbous base and a distinctive membranous ring on the stem. The gills are white and free from the stipe, and the mushroom's flesh is white. It can often be mistaken for edible white button mushrooms or other similar species, so it is essential to be cautious when foraging for wild mushrooms. Consuming even a small amount of Amanita ocreata can have serious health consequences, so it is best to avoid consuming it altogether.

Foxglove

digitalis grandiflora [DIH-JIH-tuh-lis GRAN-dih-FLOR-uh]

Yellow foxglove, or large yellow foxglove, is a species of flowering plant in the family **Plantaginaceae**. It is native to Europe and western Asia but has been introduced to other parts of the world as an ornamental plant. This biennial or perennial herbaceous plant can grow up to 1.5 meters tall and produces clusters of showy, bell-shaped, yellow flowers. The leaves are large, soft, and hairy, forming a basal rosette in the first year and developing a stem in the second year. While it is prized for its ornamental value, Digitalis grandiflora is also known for its toxic traits. All parts of the plant contain cardiac glycosides, which can be deadly if ingested in large quantities. Poisoning symptoms include vomiting, diarrhea, irregular heartbeat, and even death.

M onkshood
Aconitum napellus [UH-KOH-NUH-TUHM NUH-PEL-US]

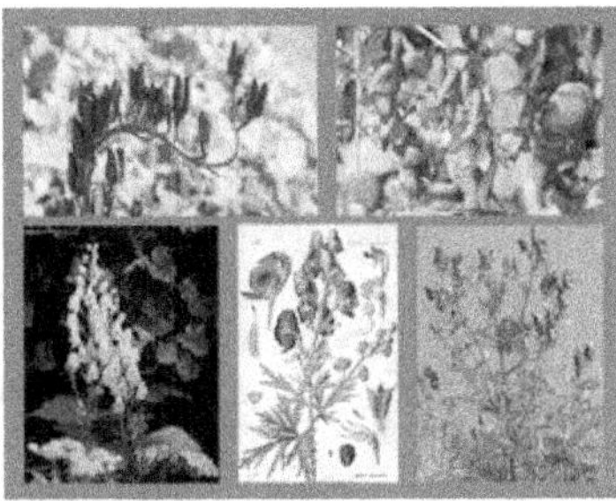

Monkshood is a flowering plant native to mountainous regions of Europe and Asia. It is also known by other common names such as wolfsbane, devil's helmet, and queen of poisons. The plant grows to about 1-2 meters tall and has a distinctive blue-purple coloration. The flowers are helmet-shaped with a hood-like upper sepal, and the leaves are deeply divided with a palmate shape. It contains a group of toxic alkaloids that affect the nervous system and the heart. Ingestion of any part of the plant can result in various symptoms, such as nausea, vomiting, paralysis, and even death. Therefore, it is essential to exercise caution when handling this plant.

Pennyroyal

Mentha pulegium [MEN-THUH PYOO-LEE-JEE-UM]

Pennyroyal oil is extracted from the leaves of the pennyroyal plant, which is in the **Lamiaceae** (mint) family. Pennyroyal oil has had many medicinal uses in folklore for at least 2000 years. Because of its strong spearmint fragrance was used as an herb to flavor teas and food and as an insecticide. It is most notable for its use to induce menstruation and abortion. Using pennyroyal oil has led to severe adverse reactions - and even death.

Pennyroyal oil contains pulegone, which is highly toxic, particularly to the liver. Ingestion can initially lead to gastrointestinal distress, such as nausea, vomiting, and abdominal pain. Later on, it can lead to failure of the liver and kidneys, resulting in bleeding, seizures, multiple organ failure, and death.

There is no antidote for pennyroyal oil poisoning. Thus, prevention and early treatment are essential.

R osary Pea

Abrus precatorius [AY-BRUHS PREE-KAY-TOR-EE-UHS]

The rosary pea, prayer bead, or jequirity bean is a plant species in many tropical regions worldwide, including Africa, Asia, and South America. It is a perennial vine that can grow up to 5 meters long, with distinctive reddish-purple flowers and pods containing seeds. The seeds are smooth and glossy with a black and red coloration, making them attractive as decorative beads, hence their common names. However, they are also highly toxic due to abrin, a protein that can cause severe illness and even death if ingested, inhaled, or handled. It's considered one of the world's most toxic plants, and caution should be exercised when handling it.

Jimsonweed

Datura stramonium [DUH-TOO-RUH STRUH-MOH-NEE-UHM]

Jimsonweed is a highly toxic and hallucinogenic plant native to North America but has since been introduced to other regions worldwide. This plant can grow up to 5 feet tall and is easily recognizable by its large, trumpet-shaped white or pale purple flowers and spiky, egg-shaped seed pods containing numerous tiny black seeds. It's common in fields, waste places, and roadsides and is considered invasive in many areas. All parts of the plant, including the leaves, seeds, and flowers, contain toxic compounds such as atropine, scopolamine, and hyoscyamine, which can cause hallucinations, delirium, tachycardia, and respiratory depression. Ingesting even a small amount of this plant can be fatal, making it essential to avoid contact with or ingestion of Datura stramonium.

PART NINE
THE WILD KITCHEN
COOKING WITH CALIFORNIA'S BOUNTY OF WILD EDIBLE PLANTS

Cooking with the foraged edible plants you harvested in California is an experience unlike any other. Whether savoring the delicate flavors of miner's lettuce in a simple salad or using fennel fronds to add a bright, anise-like note to a seafood dish, incorporating wild edible plants into your cooking opens up a world of culinary possibilities.

These plants are packed with nutrients and burst with fresh flavor, offering a unique connection to the land and the seasons. From the tartness of sorrel to the earthy sweetness of wild mushrooms, each ingredient has a story to tell, reflecting the unique terroir and climate of California's varied landscapes.

Cooking with foraged edible plants also offers an opportunity to learn about the natural world and explore the beauty and bounty of the land around you. Whether harvesting wild greens from a local park or gathering mushrooms in the woods, foraging is a way to connect with nature and learn about the land's many gifts.

So why not incorporate some of California's wild edible plants into your cooking? From delicate herbs to hearty roots, there's a world of flavor and nutrition waiting to be discovered, and each dish is an opportunity to explore the natural world in a new and delicious way.

Please enjoy the included recipes as a start to your new lifestyle.

Apple Brown Butter Bay Leaf Spice Cookies

Gluten-Free. Makes about 32 cookies.

Ingredients:

- 1 1/2 cups apple juice
- 1 cup baked apple chips, crushed into 1/4-inch pieces
- 1 tablespoon ground flax meal
- 1/2 cup + 2 tablespoons unsalted butter
- 3 fresh bay leaves
- 1/2 cup + 3 tablespoons sweet rice flour
- 1/4 cup + 2 tablespoons tapioca flour (sometimes called tapioca starch)
- 1/4 cup + 1 tablespoon teff flour
- 2 tablespoons buckwheat flour
- 2 tablespoons millet flour
- 1/2 teaspoon sea salt
- 1/2 teaspoon baking soda
- 1/2 teaspoon baking powder
- 1 teaspoon cinnamon
- 3/4 teaspoon ground ginger
- 1/4 teaspoon nutmeg
- 1/4 teaspoon fresh ground black pepper
- 1/2 cup + 2 tablespoons dark brown sugar
- 3/4 cup granulated white sugar divided
- 1 large egg
- 2 teaspoon vanilla extract

Method:

1. Place the apple juice and crushed apple chips into a medium saucepan and turn to high heat. Stirring constantly, boil the apple juice and apple chips until the apple chips have absorbed all the liquid, about 7 to 10 minutes. Once all the liquid has been absorbed, turn off the heat and stir in the flax meal. Set aside to cool.
2. Place the butter and bay leaves in a large saucepan (preferably with a silver bottom) and cook on medium-high heat until the fat particles of the butter start to brown and smell fragrant and nutty. Turn the heat off and continue to stir to cool the brown butter for a minute or two. Pour into a large heat-proof bowl, discarding the bay leaves.
3. Place the flour, salt, baking soda, baking powder, and spices in a medium bowl and stir vigorously with a balloon whisk until uniform in color.
4. Place the brown sugar and 100 grams of the white sugar (reserving 50 g of the sugar for later) in the bowl of a standing mixer fitted with that paddle attachment. Pour the brown butter into the bowl with the sugar and beat on medium speed for 30 seconds.
5. Add the egg and vanilla extract and beat on medium speed for another 30 seconds or until the batter lightens.
6. Add the dry ingredients and slowly turn the mixer on low until the dry ingredients are incorporated, and a dough starts to form.
7. Add the apples to the mixture and beat on medium speed until incorporated.

8. Place the dough in a refrigerator for an hour to chill. Once the dough has chilled, preheat the oven to 350°F and line a baking sheet with parchment paper. Spoon out a rounded tablespoon of dough and form it into a ball. Roll the dough in the reserved sugar and place it on the lined baking sheet.
9. Continue with the remaining dough, spacing the cookies apart by 2 inches.
10. Bake for 13-15 minutes or until the edges are golden brown and crisp.
11. Cool on the sheet for 10 minutes before moving the cookies to a wire sheet to cool completely.

Black Currant Sorbet

Ingredients:

- 2 cups fresh black currants
- 1 cup sugar
- 1 cup water
- 1/4 cup fresh lemon juice

Method:

1. Rinse the black currants and remove any stems or leaves.
2. Combine the sugar and water in a small saucepan and bring to a boil, stirring until the sugar dissolves. Reduce the heat and let simmer for a few minutes until the mixture thickens slightly.
3. Add the black currants to the sugar syrup and simmer for 10-15 minutes, occasionally stirring, until the fruit breaks down and the mixture thickens.
4. Remove from heat and let cool to room temperature.
5. Once cooled, transfer the black currant mixture to a blender and blend until smooth.
6. Strain the mixture through a fine-mesh sieve into a large bowl to remove any seeds or pulp.
7. Stir in the fresh lemon juice and mix well.
8. Transfer the mixture to an ice cream maker and churn according to the manufacturer's instructions until the sorbet is firm.
9. Once churned, transfer the sorbet to a freezer-safe container and freeze until ready to serve.

This black currant sorbet is the perfect refreshing dessert for a hot summer day. The sweet and tangy flavors of the black currants pair perfectly with the bright and zesty lemon juice, creating a delicious and refreshing treat that will impress your guests. Enjoy!

Braised Chicken Thighs with Bay Leaf

Makes 2 servings.

Ingredients:

- 4 chicken thighs
- 1 small onion
- 2 cloves of garlic
- 1-2 bay leaves
- oil
- salt & pepper

Method:

Wash chicken and remove excess fat.

Season the presentation side of the chicken with salt and pepper. Warm up some oil in a pot.

Place chicken in the pot and season the opposite side with salt and pepper. Braise for a few minutes on each side.

In the meantime, small dice of onion and fine dice of garlic.

Remove chicken from pot. Add a bit more oil, and deglaze the bottom of the pot with a wooden spoon.

Add onion and garlic and sauté until golden. You may want to do this at a low temperature, so the onion and garlic don't burn.

Add 1/4 cup of water and bay leaves, and stir it. Increase heat and add chicken. Pour some of the juice on top. Bring to a boil. Slightly lower the temperature and cook uncovered for about half an hour or until the chicken is done. Halfway through the cooking process, flip the chicken, so both sides cook in the juices.

Place chicken in a serving dish and pour sauce on top.

Bull Kelp Broth

Bull kelp broth can be used as a base for soups, stews, and other dishes or enjoyed as a warm, comforting beverage. The broth is rich in minerals, vitamins, and other nutrients and has a subtle, slightly sweet flavor.

Ingredients:

- 1-2 large bull kelp fronds
- 8 cups water
- 1 onion, chopped
- 2 garlic cloves, chopped
- 2 carrots, chopped
- 2 celery stalks, chopped
- 1 teaspoon salt
- 1 teaspoon black peppercorns
- 1 bay leaf

Instructions:

1. Rinse the bull kelp fronds under cold water to remove any debris. Use kitchen shears to cut the fronds into small pieces.
2. Combine the bull kelp, water, onion, garlic, carrots, celery, salt, peppercorns, and bay leaf in a large pot. Bring the mixture to a boil over high heat.
3. Reduce the heat to low and simmer the broth for 2-3 hours, stirring occasionally. The longer the broth simmers, the more flavorful it will be.
4. Strain the broth through a fine-mesh sieve, pressing down on the solids to extract as much liquid as possible.
5. Let the broth cool to room temperature, then transfer it to airtight containers and refrigerate or freeze until ready to use.

Candied Wild Flowers

Candied flowers are beautiful, edible flowers coated with a thin layer of egg white and sugar to preserve them. Candied or crystallized flowers add a delicate floral flavor and an attractive appearance to any dessert.

Ingredients:

- 1 large egg white at room temperature
- 1 teaspoon water
- 1 to 2 cups edible flowers
- 1/2 cup superfine sugar

Method:

1. Add the water to the egg white and whisk it gently with a fork or small whisk until a few bubbles appear.
2. Working with one flower at a time, dip the paintbrush in the beaten egg white and gently paint all the petals on the front of the flower.
3. Turn the flower over and paint the back of the petals as well. All the surfaces must be covered so that the flowers are adequately preserved.
4. Hold the flower over the bowl of refined sugar and sprinkle the top with a thin, even layer of sugar. Turn the blossom over and sprinkle the bottom with sugar as well.
5. If there are large clumps of sugar anywhere, dust them off gently so that only a thin, even layer of sugar remains on the flower.
6. Place the flower on a wire drying rack to dry completely. Smooth the petals out and arrange it how you would like—once it is dry, it can no longer be moved, so take the time to get it to look its best.
7. Repeat brushing the flowers with egg white, covering them with sugar, and arranging them on the drying rack until they have been candied.
8. Allow the flowers to sit at room temperature until they are completely dry. Depending on the humidity in your house, this can take anywhere from 4 to 24 hours or longer. When they are finished, the petals will be stiff.

Cascade Bilberry Tart

Ingredients:

- 1 1/2 cups all-purpose flour
- 1/2 cup unsalted butter, chilled and cubed
- 1/4 cup granulated sugar
- 1/4 tsp salt
- 2-3 tbsp ice water
- 3 cups fresh cascade bilberries
- 1/4 cup granulated sugar
- 1 tbsp cornstarch
- 1 tbsp lemon juice
- 1/4 tsp cinnamon
- 1 egg, beaten
- Coarse sugar for sprinkling

Instructions:

1. Pulse the flour, butter, sugar, and salt in a food processor until the mixture resembles coarse sand.
2. Add the ice water, one tablespoon at a time, and pulse until the dough comes together.
3. Gather the dough into a ball, flatten it into a disk, and wrap it in plastic wrap. Chill for at least 30 minutes.
4. Preheat the oven to 375°F.
5. Toss the cascade bilberries, sugar, cornstarch, lemon juice, and cinnamon in a mixing bowl.
6. Roll out the dough on a lightly floured surface to fit a 9-inch tart pan. Trim the edges and prick the bottom with a fork.
7. Spread the bilberry mixture evenly over the crust.
8. Brush the edges of the crust with the beaten egg and sprinkle with coarse sugar.
9. Bake for 30-35 minutes, until the crust is golden and the filling is bubbly.
10. Allow the tart to cool slightly before slicing and serving.

This cascade bilberry tart is a delicious and elegant dessert showcasing these unique berries' delicate and sweet flavors. Enjoy!

Cauliflower mushroom quiche

Ingredients:

- 1 9-inch pie crust
- 3 tablespoons butter
- 1 pound cauliflower mushroom, sliced
- 1 small onion, chopped
- 4 large eggs
- 1 cup milk
- 1/2 cup heavy cream
- 1/2 cup grated Parmesan cheese
- 1/2 teaspoon salt
- 1/4 teaspoon black pepper

Method:

1. Preheat the oven to 375°F (190°C).
2. Place the pie crust in a 9-inch pie dish and set aside.
3. In a large skillet, melt the butter over medium-high heat. Add the sliced cauliflower mushroom and chopped onion, then sauté until the mushroom is tender and lightly browned, about 8 to 10 minutes. Remove from heat.
4. Whisk together the eggs, milk, heavy cream, Parmesan cheese, salt, and black pepper in a mixing bowl.
5. Add the sautéed mushroom mixture to the pie crust, spreading it evenly.
6. Pour the egg mixture over the mushroom mixture.
7. Bake for 35-40 minutes, or until the quiche is set and the top is golden brown.

Allow the quiche to cool for a few minutes before slicing and serving.

This cauliflower mushroom quiche is a tasty and easy way to enjoy the unique flavor and texture of Sparassis crispa. Enjoy!

Cleavers Facial Wash

This wash will help to tighten up loose skin folds. Gradual results should become evident within two weeks. You should begin to see a brightening and smoothing of the skin, making it look less tired.

Ingredients:

- 1 Quart water
- 3 1/2 Tablespoons Dried cleavers

Method:

- Bring a quart of water to a boil.
- Remove from heat and add dried cleavers.
- Cover and steep for 40 min.

To Use: Soak a washcloth or small terrycloth hand in the chilled tea, then wash the face and neck or apply as a compress over the face for up to 10 minutes several times daily.

Crabapple Hot Pepper Jelly

Makes 4 (8 oz.) jars.

Ingredients:

- 2 pounds crab apples (1 kg.)
- 1 1/2 cups water
- red wine vinegar
- 3 3/4 cups granulated sugar
- 1 cup sweet green peppers
- 1/3 cup hot peppers

Method:

1. In a Dutch oven, combine apples with water. Cover and bring slowly to simmer; cook until apples are very soft. Pour into a colander lined with a square of dampened muslin and place over a deep bowl. Weight down with a saucer and heavy can. Let stand until the dripping stops. Discard pulp.
2. Pour collected juice into liquid measure; add enough vinegar to make 3 cups. Combine in a saucepan with sugar. Bring to a boil, stirring. Add peppers; boil briskly for 8-10 minutes or until set. Stir for 7 minutes to prevent floating peppers.
3. Pour jelly into hot, sterilized 8 oz. (1/2 pint) preserving jars. Seal with two-piece canning lids. Let cool and refrigerate. For long-term unrefrigerated storage, the process is in a boiling-water bath for 5 minutes immediately after sealing jars.

Notes:

Crab apple pectin gives this hot pepper jelly a good set. Mix and match hot peppers for color and degree of heat.

When chopping hot peppers, wear gloves and don't touch your face or eyes.

Double Dock Dip

Makes 3 1/2 cups

Ingredients:

- 1/2 lb. burdock root, peeled and sliced into thin coins
- 8 cups of curly dock leaves, cut into bite-sized pieces
- 1 sweet onion, cut into small cubes
- 6 cloves garlic, minced
- 10 oz grated mozzarella cheese, 2 oz set aside
- 4 oz freshly grated parmesan cheese or a mix of parmesan and Romano
- 2 oz freshly grated asiago cheese
- 1 cup sour cream
- 4 oz cream cheese, softened and cubed
- 1 tbs. cumin
- 1 tsp. cayenne
- 2 tsp. freshly ground black pepper
- Kosher salt
- paprika
- butter or olive oil

Method:

1. Preheat oven to 375.
2. Add your thinly sliced burdock to a saucepan and cover with water. Add water to cover and a pinch of salt. Cover and bring to a boil. Continue to boil until your burdock is tender. This can take around 30 minutes, depending on how thinly you slice.
3. While the burdock is cooking, add a drizzle of olive oil or a pat of butter to a sauté pan. Add your minced garlic, cubed onion, and a pinch of salt. Continue to sauté till the onion is translucent and tender, about 10 minutes. Then remove from heat and set aside.
4. Add the curly dock and water to cover a large saucepan. Bring to a boil and cook until the greens are fully cooked. They will turn olive green because oxalic acid responds to heat. This is normal and what you want to happen.
5. Drain the greens and place them in a large mixing bowl. Add your onion, garlic, mozzarella (except for the 2 oz you reserved), parmesan, asiago, sour cream, cream cheese, cumin, cayenne, black pepper, and half a teaspoon of salt. Mix thoroughly.
6. When the burdock is tender, drain and run under cold water to cool.
7. Cut your burdock slices into small cubes or a large mince. Add to the cheese and greens, and mix.
8. Grease an oven-proof dish. A 9 x 13 glass or ceramic baking dish is ideal. Pour in your mixture and spread it out evenly.
9. Sprinkle the reserved mozzarella evenly over the top. Then dust lightly with paprika. This will mix with the melted cheese into a beautiful rust color.

10. Place in the oven and bake at 375 for 40 minutes, until the top cheese is melted
    and browned, and the inside is a gooey, cheesy, delicious treat.

Enjoy double dock dip with veggies, pita points, tortilla chips, etc. If you have left-
overs, it microwaves well.

E elgrass soup

Ingredients:

- 4 cups fresh Eelgrass, washed and chopped into small pieces
- 1 onion, chopped
- 2 cloves garlic, minced
- 2 carrots, chopped
- 2 celery stalks, chopped
- 6 cups vegetable broth or water
- 1 teaspoon dried thyme
- 1 teaspoon dried oregano
- Salt and black pepper, to taste
- 2 tablespoons olive oil

Instructions:

1. Wash the Eelgrass thoroughly and chop it into small pieces.
2. In a large soup pot, heat the olive oil over medium heat. Add the onion, garlic, carrots, celery, and sauté until the vegetables are soft and the onion is translucent.
3. Add the Eelgrass to the pot and stir to combine with the vegetables.
4. Add the vegetable broth or water to the pot and the thyme, oregano, salt, and black pepper. Bring the soup to a boil.
5. Reduce the heat and simmer the soup for 30-40 minutes or until the Eelgrass is tender.
6. Remove the pot from the heat and use an immersion blender or transfer the soup to a blender to puree the mixture until smooth.
7. Return the soup to the pot and reheat it if necessary.
8. Taste the soup and adjust the seasoning if needed.
9. Serve the Eelgrass soup hot, and enjoy!

Note: You can add other ingredients to the soup, such as potatoes, sweet potatoes, other vegetables, or any meat, to create your unique recipe.

G ooseberry and Bay Leaf Jam

Ingredients:

- 2 1/2 cups gooseberries, cleaned and stalks removed
- 2 /2 cups jam sugar
- 3 fresh bay leaves
- 1 lemon juiced

Method:

1. Wash the gooseberries, and leave them to drain in a colander for 10 minutes.
2. Place the gooseberries, sugar, and bay leaf into a heavy base saucepan, and place over medium heat. Gently melt the sugar. Once the sugar has dissolved, turn the heat up and bring it to a vigorous boil.
3. Wash the edges of the pan with a pastry brush dipped in hot water; this will prevent the jam from crystallizing. Only stir a couple of times the jam while is boiling. Continuous stirring will encourage crystallization; do not let your jam burn. Skim any impurities from the surface as the temperature rises.
4. Boil the jam for about 20- 25 minutes, temperature 104°C – 107°C; this is the ideal setting point for the jam.
5. When you reach the correct temperature, remove the jam from the heat and stir in the lemon juice.
6. Have your jam jars ready, cleaned, and sterilized, as decanting the hot jam as soon as possible is essential.
7. Cool the jam jars, clean and label them.

Notes:

Crystallization of Jam:

There are three reasons for the jam to crystallize.

1. If the sugar and fruit starts to boil before all the "raw" sugar crystals have dissolved.
2. Once the sugar had dissolved, and the jam reached the vigorous boiling stage, you did not wash the edges with a pastry brush dipped in hot water. As the "raw" sugar crystals get stuck to the edge of the pan and fall back into the boiling syrup, the larger un-dissolved crystals accumulate molecules, encouraging the growth of large crystals known as crystallization.
3. You should not stir boiling jam, or sugar syrup for that matter, too much. If you continuously stir the boiling syrup, it knocks the sugar crystals together and encourages the formation of larger crystals, and crystallization sets in once cooled.

Sterilizing the jars:

This is one of the most crucial tasks; you should never cut corners. If you do not do this properly, your jam might become moldy and ferment sooner than expected. Preheat the oven to 225°F. Wash the jars in hot soapy water; do not dry them with a tea towel. Place the damp jars and lids on a clean baking tray; try not to touch the jars and lids on the insides. Place them in the preheated oven for about 40 minutes. Let the jars cool slightly before you scoop in the jam. Take extra care when sterilizing the jars. If they are overheated, they might explode. Never pour cold liquid into hot glass jars. You will end up with broken glass.

Hedgehog Mushrooms and Bacon Pasta

Makes 4 servings

Ingredients:

- 10 ½ - 14 ounces dried penne pasta
- 4 ½ ounces bacon
- 1/2 tablespoon olive oil
- 1 clove garlic, minced
- 1 small onion, finely chopped
- 1 sprig thyme
- 1 tablespoon Fresh oregano
- 7 ½ ounces fresh hedgehog mushrooms, cubed
- 7/8 cup heavy cream
- 1 cup pasta cooking water
- 1 tablespoon butter
- 1 ½ ounces freshly grated parmesan cheese
- 1 handful of parsley, chopped

Method:

1. Cook pasta according to packaged directions.
2. Save 1 cup of pasta cooking water once the pasta is cooked.
3. In a large frying pan over medium-high heat, cook the bacon until crispy. Remove and set aside bacon.
4. Reduce heat and add olive oil, onion, and garlic to the bacon grease.
5. Stir constantly for 2 minutes until the onion and garlic have softened.
6. Add thyme, oregano, and mushrooms, and cook for 10 minutes.
7. Add 1 cup of pasta water and heavy cream, and bring to a gentle boil. Let cook for 1-2 minutes.
8. Add cooked pasta, and continue cooking until the sauce thickens and sticks to the pasta. Add butter and parmesan cheese, and stir well.
9. Serve with cooked bacon and chopped parsley.

Iced Blueberry Labrador Tea

Ingredients:

- 8 cups of brewed Labrador tea
- 2 cups blueberries (fresh or thawed)
- 1/4 cup packed brown sugar
- 1 cup water
- 1 tablespoon lemon juice

Method:

1. In a large saucepan, bring blueberries and water to a boil. Reduce heat and simmer, often stirring, until blueberries break down, about 5 minutes.
2. Add blueberries to the brewed Labrador tea.
3. Add brown sugar to the blueberry tea mixture; stir and allow to cool to room temperature for about 30 minutes.
4. Refrigerate until cold, about 2 hours.
5. Strain the mixture through a cheesecloth-lined sieve into a pitcher.
6. Stir in lemon juice.

Lamb's Quarters Tincture

Ingredients:

- Fresh or dried Lamb's Quarters leaves and stems
- 80- to 100-proof alcohol (such as vodka or brandy)
- Glass jar with a tight-fitting lid
- Cheesecloth or fine-mesh strainer
- Amber dropper bottles for storage

Method:

1. Harvest fresh Lamb's Quarters leaves and stems or use dried ones. If using fresh, wash and dry them thoroughly. If using dried, crumble them into small pieces.
2. Fill a glass jar about 2/3 full with the Lamb's Quarters leaves and stems.
3. Pour the alcohol over the Lamb's Quarters until it covers the herb by about an inch.
4. Put the lid on the jar and shake it vigorously for a few minutes.
5. Store the jar in a cool, dark place for 4-6 weeks, shaking it daily to help release the plant's medicinal constituents into the alcohol.
6. After 4-6 weeks, strain the tincture through a cheesecloth or fine-mesh strainer into a clean glass jar.
7. Press the plant material to extract as much of the liquid as possible.
8. Transfer the tincture to amber dropper bottles for storage.

The recommended dosage for Lamb's Quarter's tincture is usually 30-60 drops up to three times daily. It's always best to consult a healthcare practitioner before using herbal remedies.

Nightshade Jam

Harvest your nightshade from a bush area you know is organic and spray-free.

Ensure the berries are fully ripe (dark purple/black color). Don't harvest unripe (green or light purple color) as that is poisonous.

Ingredients:

- 500g of fresh ripe nightshade berries
- 400g of quality raw sugar
- 1 tbsp of lemon juice

Method:

1. Remove the berries from the stems with your hands or isolate them while you forage them. Remove any bits of leaf and stalk.
2. Gently wash the berries with fresh water. Be careful because these berries are porous.
3. Place the berries in a heavy-based pan and gently crush with a potato masher or squeeze with your hand, just enough to release some of the juices. Turn the pan on.
4. Add the sugar and lemon juice to the pan and leave to simmer on low heat. Allow for 5 minutes of bubbles. Keep stirring to prevent the jam from sticking to the bottom of the pan.
5. Cook down for around 20 minutes. Allow about 5 minutes of bubbles to come while simmering.
6. Put the jam into clean jars. The jam will keep in a cool dark place for one year.

Once opened, keep it refrigerated.

Northern Dewberry Syrup

Ingredients:

- 4 cups of northern dewberries
- 2 cups of water
- 2 cups of granulated sugar
- 1 tablespoon of lemon juice

Method:

1. Rinse the northern dewberries under cold water to remove any dirt or debris. Pat them dry with a paper towel.
2. In a medium saucepan, combine the northern dewberries and water. Bring the mixture to a boil over medium heat, then reduce the heat to low and simmer for about 15 minutes, stirring occasionally.
3. Remove the saucepan from the heat and let the mixture cool for a few minutes.
4. Strain the mixture through a fine-mesh sieve into a large bowl, pressing down on the solids to extract as much juice as possible. Discard the solids.
5. Return the strained liquid to the saucepan and add the sugar and lemon juice. Stir to combine.
6. Bring the mixture to a boil over medium heat, stirring occasionally, then reduce the heat to low and simmer for about 20-25 minutes or until the mixture has thickened to a syrupy consistency.
7. Remove the saucepan from the heat and let the mixture cool for a few minutes.
8. Pour the syrup into a sterilized jar and let it cool to room temperature before storing it in the refrigerator for up to one month.

Enjoy your homemade northern dewberry syrup on pancakes, waffles, ice cream, or as a sweetener for your favorite beverages!

Yellow Rocketcress Pesto

Rocketcress is delicious with pasta and as an appetizer on bread or toast.

Ingredients:

- 2 handfuls of Landcress
- Olive oil
- A handful of Pine Nuts or Cashews
- A handful of Parmesan cheese
- Pepper / Salt
- Hand blender

Method:

1. Roast the pine nuts to golden brown in a skillet before combining them with the other ingredients.
2. Combine the cress, pine nuts, cashews, and Parmesan in a bowl with oil.
3. Add small amounts of oil while blending with the hand blender until smooth.
4. Taste the pesto and season it with a bit of pepper or salt.

*Notes: When using a block of Parmesan cheese, make sure you rasp it beforehand.

R owan Berry Pie

For the crust:

- 1 1/2 cups all-purpose flour
- 1/2 cup unsalted butter, cold and cubed
- 1/4 cup granulated sugar
- 1/4 teaspoon salt
- 1 egg yolk
- 2-3 tablespoons ice water

For the filling:

- 2 cups Rowan berries, washed and stemmed
- 1/2 cup granulated sugar
- 1/4 cup all-purpose flour
- 1/4 teaspoon salt
- 1 tablespoon unsalted butter, melted

Instructions:

1. Preheat the oven to 375°F (190°C).
2. Mix the flour, sugar, and salt for the crust in a large bowl.
3. Add the cold cubed butter and cut it using a pastry cutter or a fork until the mixture resembles coarse crumbs.
4. In a small bowl, whisk together the egg yolk and ice water.
5. Add the egg mixture to the flour mixture and stir with a fork until the dough comes together.
6. Form the dough into a ball and flatten it into a disk. Wrap it in plastic wrap and chill it in the refrigerator for at least 30 minutes.
7. Roll out the chilled dough on a floured surface to fit a 9-inch tart pan. Press the dough into the pan and trim the edges.
8. Mix the Rowan berries, sugar, flour, and salt in a separate bowl for the filling.
9. Pour the filling into the prepared crust and spread it out evenly.
10. Drizzle the melted butter over the top of the filling.
11. Bake the tart for 35-40 minutes until the crust is golden brown and the filling is bubbling.
12. Allow the tart to cool for at least 10 minutes before slicing and serving.

Enjoy your delicious Rowan berry pie!

Sautéed Black Nightshade

Prep: 15 minutes.

Makes 3 servings.

Ingredients:

- 1 bunch (medium-sized) Black Nightshade
- 2 Onions (finely chopped)
- 3-4 Red Chillies
- 3-4 Tablespoons Grated Coconut
- 1/2 teaspoon Mustard Seeds
- 200-250 ml Water
- To taste Salt
- As required Oil

Method:

1. Clean and wash the spinach. Then chop it unevenly.
2. Now heat the oil in a pan, and crackle the mustard seeds. Add chopped onion and red chili and sauté the mixture.
3. Add water, salt, and chopped spinach.
4. When the leaves get a little cooked, mix them slightly.
5. When the mixture has little water, add the grated coconut.
6. Some prefer a soggy mixture, and others may like dry stuff.
7. Serve according to your taste.

Note: Add more chopped onions and grated coconut to reduce the bitterness in the Black Nightshade.

S eacoast Angelica root tincture

Ingredients:

- Fresh Seacoast Angelica root (chopped)
- 80- to 100-proof alcohol (such as vodka or brandy)
- Glass jar with a tight-fitting lid
- Cheesecloth or fine-mesh strainer
- Amber dropper bottles for storage

Method:

1. Collect fresh Seacoast Angelica roots from a reputable source, preferably during the fall when the plant's energy is concentrated in its roots.
2. Clean the roots and chop them into small pieces.
3. Fill a glass jar about 2/3 full with the chopped Seacoast Angelica roots.
4. Pour enough alcohol over the roots to cover them by about an inch.
5. Put the lid on the jar and shake it well to ensure the alcohol is evenly distributed.
6. Store the jar in a cool, dark place for 4-6 weeks, shaking it daily to help release the plant's medicinal constituents into the alcohol.
7. After 4-6 weeks, strain the tincture through a cheesecloth or fine-mesh strainer into a clean glass jar.
8. Press the plant material to extract as much of the liquid as possible.
9. Transfer the tincture to amber dropper bottles for storage.

The recommended dosage for Seacoast Angelica tincture is usually 20-40 drops up to three times daily. It's always best to consult a healthcare practitioner before using herbal remedies.

CONCLUSION

Wild edible plants are abundant in California and offer many culinary and nutritional benefits. From the towering redwoods of the north to the sun-drenched deserts of the south, California's diverse landscape is home to a remarkable variety of edible plants that have sustained humans for millennia.

Through this book, we have explored just a tiny sampling of the many edible plants found in California. From the Fourwing Saltbush to the delicate miner's lettuce, these plants offer a range of flavors and nutritional profiles that can be enjoyed in a variety of ways.

As we have seen, wild edible plants offer a host of nutritional benefits, including vitamins, minerals, fiber, and antioxidants. These benefits can help support overall health and wellness and may even protect against chronic diseases like heart disease, cancer, and diabetes.

However, it is essential to approach wild edible plants with caution and respect. Some plants can be toxic or cause allergic reactions, and it is necessary to correctly identify and prepare any wild edible plants before consuming them. Foraging should also be done sustainably, preserving the health of the environment and the plants themselves.

As we progress, it is important to continue learning about and appreciating California's many wild edible plants. By doing so, we can deepen our connection to the land and the rich cultural traditions that have grown up around wild edible plants in this region.

To that end, supporting and promoting the conservation of California's natural habitats and their diverse plant species is essential. By preserving these habitats and the plants that grow within them, we can ensure that future generations can learn from and enjoy the bounty of wild edible plants California offers.

In conclusion, this book is just a starting point for exploring California's many wild edible plants. By continuing to learn, appreciate, and protect these plants and the environments in which they grow, we can honor this region's rich cultural and natural heritage and sustain a thriving and diverse food culture for years to come.

PART TEN
APPENDIX

THE UNIVERSAL EDIBILITY TEST

CAUTION: THIS TEST DOES NOT APPLY TO MUSHROOMS.

If you are in an unfamiliar area or a survival situation, you may be unable to identify edible plants. In this case, you'd want to use the universal edibility test. As the name suggests, this test will help determine whether a plant is edible. It should only be used as a last resort, as you should ideally never be in a situation where you can't find an identifiable plant or mushroom. Always check the edibility of your harvest, even if you're sure it's safe to eat. This is important when foraging and identifying an edible plant you've never tried before.

Everyone will come across this scenario at some point. Even if you're confident that you've identified an edible plant, only try a small amount first. Even something safe to eat can make you feel unwell if you have digestive issues. Sometimes a food you haven't tried before doesn't agree with you, and you don't want to discover this after having a large portion. It's also possible to have an undiagnosed food allergy. Suppose you eat a lot of plant food on an empty stomach. In that case, you can quickly get cramps, nausea, diarrhea, or other gastrointestinal issues. An upset stomach is a quick way to ruin an otherwise enjoyable foraging trip.

Step 1: Fast for eight hours. You likely haven't eaten for at least eight hours in a survival situation like this. Still, it's essential to start on an empty stomach so that you know whether or not the plant you are testing is what has made you unwell. You can and should drink plenty of clean water, if possible.

Step 2: Check for common poisonous traits. Most toxic plants have distinguishing characteristics that are unlikely to be found on edible plants. These include shiny, waxy leaves, spines, fine hairs, milky sap, umbrella-shaped flowers, and green or white berries. If it looks like dill or parsley, avoid it, and steer clear of anything that smells like almonds. Not every plant with these characteristics is toxic, edible dandelions have milky sap, for example, but it's an excellent rule of thumb. Rule out anything with those traits.

Step 3: Once you find a plant without any of those traits, ensure you can find plenty of specimens. Remember, the edibility test takes time, so there's not much point in going through the whole process if you can't find any more plants of that type. When you find a likely plant, break it into sections: flower, leaf, stem, etc. Not every plant part is edible, even if one part is. For example, potato tubers are edible, but the plant's stem is toxic. You will need to test every aspect of the plant individually.

Step 4: Now, it's time to start testing. Select a plant part and rub it on your skin. Most people rub it on their inner forearm, the inside of their elbow, or their outer lip. Wait for fifteen minutes. Continue with the test if you don't experience tingling, burning, or other adverse reactions. If any of the above persist, you will want to choose a different plant part.

Step 5: If all is well from the step above, do a taste test with the same plant part. Put it in your mouth and don't chew or swallow; leave it for five minutes. Spit it out and wash your mouth if you have any adverse reactions. Do the same if you taste bitterness, soapy flavors, or experience numbness. If nothing happens, continue with the test.

Step 6: Do a more extensive taste test. Now put the plant part in your mouth and chew for five minutes. Wait for any adverse effects mentioned above and spit out excess saliva (don't swallow anything yet). If everything seems okay after five minutes, swallow the plant part. Now the waiting begins. You need to fast for another eight hours before the next step.

Step 7: If you haven't experienced any digestive issues, you can prepare and eat one tablespoon of the plant part. If possible, it's usually safer to cook the plant part. If there are no poisoning symptoms after another eight hours of waiting, you can be sure this plant part is edible as you prepared. It would be best if you still didn't gorge yourself, but at least you have a relatively dependable food source. You'll reduce the chance of accidental poisoning by sticking with small amounts and waiting eight hours between tasting and eating. Suppose you have significant gastrointestinal symptoms in a survival situation, like vomiting or diarrhea. In that case, you may not be able to seek medical attention.

Plant Families

Actinidiaceae - This flowering plant family has three genera and about 355 species. They consist of shrubs, small trees, and lianas. They are primarily tropical and are particularly common in Southeast Asia.

Anacardiaceae - The cashew or sumac family of flowering plants includes 83 genera and 860 species. Several species bear drupes and sometimes produce *urushiol*, which can cause skin irritation.

Apiaceae - Known as the celery, carrot, and parsley family, or umbellifers, primarily aromatic flowering plants are named after the genus Apium.

Araliaceae - There are approximately 43 genera and about 1500 species of flowering plants in this family, most of these plants are woody, and some are herbaceous.

Asparagaceae - the asparagus family of flowering plants based on the edible garden asparagus, *Asparagus officinalis*.

Aspleniaceae - The spleenwort family **is** a family of ferns

Asteraceae - The Compositae family was first described in the year 1740. They are called daisies, sunflowers, asters, composites, or sunflowers. With more than 32,000 species and 1,900 genera, it is the world's largest flowering plant group, rivaled only by the Orchidaceae family.

Berberidaceae - Generally known as the Barberry family, this group of flowering plants contains 18 genera.

Brassicaceae - These medium-sized flowering plants are economically important. They are commonly known as the mustards, crucifers, or cabbage family.

Caryophyllaceae - The carnation family is a family of flowering plants with about 2,625 known species.

Elaeagnaceae - The Oleaster family comprises small trees and shrubs.

Ericaceae - The heath or heather family consists of flowering plants that flourish in acidic and infertile environments. Cranberries, blueberries, huckleberries, rhododendron (including azaleas), and a wide range of heaths and heathers are examples of well-known members.

Euphorbiaceae - Among flowering plants, the spurge family is one of the largest. They are also commonly known as euphorbias in English, their genus name. Most spurges are herbs, such as Euphorbia paralias, but some are shrubs or trees, particularly in the tropics.

Lamiaceae [LAY-mee-AY-see-ee] The mint or deadnettle family is aromatic in all parts. They include widely used culinary herbs like basil, mint, rosemary, sage, savory, marjoram, oregano, hyssop, thyme, lavender, and perilla. Catnip, salvia, bee balm, wild dagga, and oriental motherwort are medicinal herbs.

Malvaceae - The Mallow family of flowering plants is estimated to contain 244 genera with 4225 known species. Among the well-known members of this plant family are okra, cotton, cacao, and durian.

Menispermaceae - The moonseed family comprises 440 species, most of which are found in low-lying tropical regions, with some species also found in temperate and arid regions.

Morchellaceae -

Oxalidaceae - The wood sorrel family comprises five genera of herbaceous plants, shrubs, and small trees, with about 570 species in the Oxalis genus.

Plantaginaceae - The Plantain family and order Lamiales include common flower species such as snapdragon and foxglove.

Polygonaceae - The knotweed or smartweed-buckwheat family is an informal name for a family of flowering plants. There are about 1200 species within about 48 genera. There are members of this family worldwide, but they are most abundant in the North Temperate Zone.

Portulacaceae - The purslane family is a family of flowering plants with 115 species in one genus, Portulaca.

Ranunculaceae - the buttercup or crowfoot family is a family of over 2,000 known flowering plants in 43 genera distributed worldwide.

Rosaceae - The rose family includes 4,828 species of flowering plants.

Viburnaceae - was previously known as the Adoxaceae family and is commonly known as the Moschatel family. About 150–200 species belong to this family of flowering plants.

Plant Types

Annual [**an**-yoo-*uhl*] - Plants without a permanent woody stem. They are usually flowering garden plants or potherbs.

Deciduous [dih-**sij**-oo-uhs] - After the growing season, the plant sheds leaves and turns dormant.

Dioecious [dahy-**ee**-sh*uhs*] - having the male and female organs in separate and distinct individuals, having different sexes.

Herbaceous [hur-**bey**-sh*uhs*] - low-growing plants with soft green stems. Their above-ground growth is often seasonal.

Monoecious [muh-**nee**-shuhs] - having the stamens and the pistils in separate flowers on the same plant.

Perennial [puh-**ren**-ee-uhl] - It usually lasts for more than two years. These plants don't have a lot of woody growth.

Plant Parts

Achene [*uh*-**keen**] - a small, dry one-seeded fruit that does not open to release the seed.

Anther [**an**-ther] - the pollen-bearing part of a stamen.

Filament [**fil**-*uh*-m*uh*nt] - the stalklike portion of a stamen, supporting the anther.

Ligulate [**lig**-y*uh*-lit] - strap-shaped, such as the ray florets of daisy family plants.

Peltate [**pel**-teyt] - fixed to the stalk by the center or by some point distinctly within the margin.

Petiole [**pet**-ee-ohl] - the slender stalk by which a leaf is attached to the stem; leafstalk.

Pistil [**pis**-tl] - the ovule-bearing or seed-bearing female organ of a flower, consisting when complete of the ovary, style, and stigma.

Pith [pith] - The soft central cylinder of tissue in the plant's stem.

Sepal [**see**-p*uh*l] - The outer parts of the flower (often green and leaf-like) that enclose a developing bud.

Sessile [**ses**-il] - attached directly by its base without a stalk or peduncle.

Stamen [**stey**-m*uh*n] - the pollen-bearing organ of a flower, consisting of the filament and the anther.

Staminodia [stam-*uh*-**noh**-dee-*uh*] - A stamen that is sterile or abortive.

Whorled [wurl'd] - The arrangement of like parts around a point on an axis, such as leaves or flowers;

<u>Leaf Types</u>

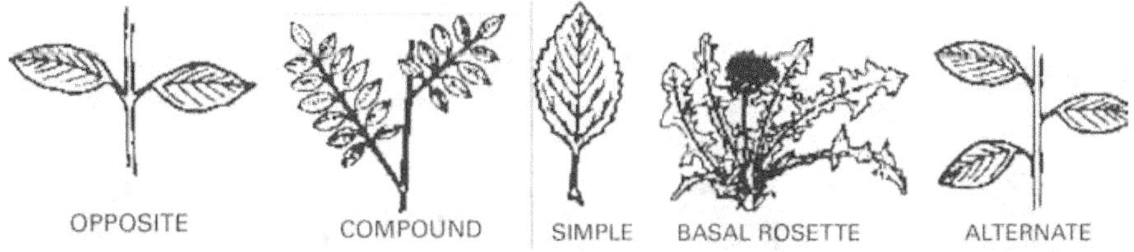

Alternate - The leaves are single at each node and spiral upwards along the stem.

Basal leaf - a leaf that grows lowest on the stem of a plant or flower.

Compound - composed of two or more leaflets that are attached to a single leaf stalk or petiole.

Opposite - When two leaves are attached at the same node, one on either side of the stem.

Palmate [**pal**-meyt] - Having four or more lobes or leaflets.

Palmately compound - A petiole's tip is attached to a leaflet.

Pinnate [**pin**-eyt] - Each side of a stalk is divided into leaflets

Rosette [roh-**zet**] - a circular arrangement of leaves or structures resembling leaves.

Simple - Leaves with a single, undivided lamina

Tripinnately compound - Leaf made up of three pinnate parts.

Leaf Shapes

Cordate [**kawr**-deyt] - heart-shaped.

Elliptical [ih-**lip**-ti-k*uh*l] - Planar, shaped like a flattened circle, symmetrical about the long and short axes, tapering equally to the tip and the base; oval.

Lanceolate [**an**-see-*uh*-leyt] - shaped like the head of a lance, having a rounded base and a tapering apex.

Long-pointed - Lying close and flat and pointing toward the plant's apex or structure.

Oblanceolate [ob-**lan**-see-*uh*-lit] - having a rounded apex and a tapering base.

Oblong [**ob**-lawng]- Having a length a few times greater than the width, with sides almost parallel and ends rounded.

Ovate [**oh**-veyt] - egg-shaped, having such a shape with a broader end at the base.

Triangular [trahy-**ang**-gy*uh*-ler] - Planar with three sides.

Wedge - narrowly triangular, wider at the apex, and tapering toward the base.

Flower Types

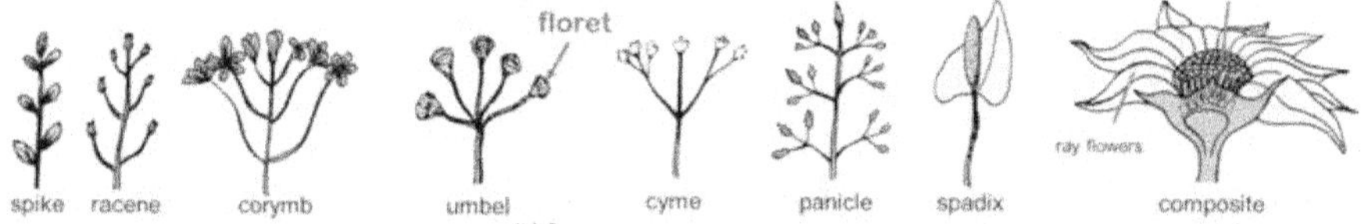

Corymb [**kawr**-imb] - a form of inflorescence in which the flowers form a flat-topped or convex cluster, the outermost flowers being the first to open.

Composite [k*uh*m-**poz**-it] is characterized by alternate, opposite, or *whorled* leaves and a whorl of bracts surrounding its flower heads. These flower heads typically extend from a disk containing tiny petal-less flowers and from the disk's rim to a ray of petals.

Cyme [sahym] - an inflorescence in which the primary axis bears a single central or terminal flower that blooms first.

Inflorescence [in-flaw-**res**-*uh*ns] - the complete flower head of a plant, including stems, stalks, bracts, and flowers.

Panicle [**pan**-i-k*uh*l] - any loose, diversely branching flower cluster.

Raceme [rey-**seem**] - a flower cluster with separate flowers attached by short equal stalks at equal distances along a central stem. The flowers at the base of the main stem develop first.

Spike [spahyk] - a type of racemose inflorescence.

Spadix [**spey**-diks] - an inflorescence consisting of a spike with a fleshy or thickened axis, usually enclosed in a spathe.

Umbel or Subumbel [**uhm**-b*uh*l] - consisting of several short flower stalks that spread from a common point, like umbrella ribs.

Seaweed

Blade - refers to the flattened and elongated portion of the seaweed that is similar to a leaf. The blade is the main photosynthetic organ of seaweed, and it is responsible for capturing light energy for photosynthesis.

Float - refers to a gas-filled bladder or sac that helps the seaweed stay afloat and near the water's surface where it can receive maximum sunlight for photosynthesis.

Stipe - the stem-like structure that supports the leafy fronds. It is the main axis of the seaweed body and is analogous to the stem of a land plant.

Holdfast - a structure that anchors the seaweed to a solid surface, such as a rock or the ocean floor. Holdfasts are a critical part of the seaweed's anatomy as they provide stability and allow the seaweed to withstand the strong currents and waves of the ocean.

Fruit/Berry

Aggregate fruit [AG-RI-GIT FROOT]- composed of a cluster of carpels belonging to the same flower as the raspberry.

Dehiscent [DIH-HIS-UHNT] - opens to release seeds or pollen

Drupe [droop] - a fleshy fruit with thin skin and a central stone containing the seed, e.g., a plum, cherry, almond, or olive.

Globoid [**gloh**-boid] - approximately globular. Globe-shaped; spherical.

Infructescence [in-fruc-TES-cence] - an aggregate fruit.

Syconium [sahy-**koh**-nee-*uh*m] - a fleshy hollow receptacle that develops into a multifruit.

Bark

Acaulescent [ak-aw-**les**-*uh*nt] - stemless

Lenticel [**len**-t*uh*-sel] - One of the many holes in a woody plant's stem that allows air to exchange between the inside and outside.

Myrmecochory - the dispersal of fruits and seeds by ants.

Elaiosome - an oil-rich body on seeds or fruits that attracts ants, which act as dispersal agents.

Medical Terms

Amygdalin [*uh*-**mig**-d*uh*-lin] - White, bitter-tasting glycosidic powder usually obtained from the leaves and seeds of plants of the genus Prunus and related genera: used mainly as an expectorant in medicine.

Anthocyanins [an-thuh-**sahy**-uh-nin] - These flavonoids are known for their pigmentation properties, responsible for fruits, vegetables, flowers, and cereals' red, purple, and blue colors.

Astringent [*uh*-**strin**-j*uh*nt] - Contracting the body's tissues or canals reduces mucus or blood discharges.

Berberine [**bur**-b*uh*-reen] - Known as an antipyretic, antibacterial, and stomachic, this crystalline, water-soluble alkaloid is derived from barberry or goldenseal.

Carotenoid [k*uh*-**rot**-n-oid] - Red or yellow pigments, similar to carotene, found in animal fat and some plants.

Cyanogenic glycosides - chemical compounds contained in foods that release hydrogen cyanide when chewed or digested.

Demulcent [dih-**muhl**-s*uh*nt] - a substance that relieves irritation of the mucous membranes in the mouth by forming a protective film.

Depurative [DEP-YUH-REY-TIV] - herbs considered to have purifying and detoxifying effects.

Flavonoids [FLEY-VUH-NOID] - An antioxidant, antiviral, anticancer, anti-inflammatory, and anti-allergenic group of water-soluble polyphenols found in plants.

Hydrocyanic acid - scientific word for cyanide.

Lutein [LOO-TEEN] - is known to have anti-inflammatory and immune-boosting properties, and is important for maintaining healthy eyes and skin.

Lycopene [LAHY-KUH-PEEN] - Red crystalline substance found in some fruits, including tomatoes and paprika.

Odontalgic [OH-DON-TAL-JUH] - toothache.

Prunasin [PRÜ-Nə-SəN] - A cyanogenic glucoside related to amygdalin found in Prunus species.

Urolithiasis [YOOR-OH-LI-**THAHY**-UH-SIS] - A disease where stones form in the urinary tract.

Urushiol [OO-**ROO**-SHEE-AWL] - The active irritant principle in several plant species in the Rhus genus.

Zeaxanthin [ZEE-UH-ZAN-THIN] - is found in the macula of the eye, where it plays a role in protecting the eye from oxidative damage and age-related macular degeneration.

. . .

Anthropogenic [AN-THR*UH*-P*UH*-JEN-IK] - caused by humans.

Decoction - concentrated herbal extracts that are made by boiling the plant material in water.

Glaucous [GLAW-K*UH*S] - covered with a whitish bloom, as a plum.

Siliceous [S*UH*-LISH-*UH*S] - growing in soil rich in silica.

Calcareous [KAL-KAIR-EE-*UH*S] - occurring on chalk or limestone.

Monoecious [M*UH*-NEE-SH*UH*S] - On the same plant, the stamens and pistils are in separate flowers.

Mucilaginous [MYOO-S*UH*-LAJ-*UH*-N*UH*S] - having a viscous or gelatinous consistency.

Shannon Warner is a long-time forager and survivalist with a deep love for the outdoors. She has spent countless hours exploring the wilderness, learning about the plants and animals that inhabit it, and honing her skills in sustainable harvesting and ethical foraging. Shannon has embarked on many adventures with her two loyal dogs by her side, from hiking and camping to hunting and fishing.

She loves sharing her extensive knowledge of the edible plants that grow in the wild, helping readers identify, harvest, and use them for culinary and medicinal purposes. Her passion for the subject is evident on every page, and her clear and concise writing style makes it easy for even beginners to understand.

One of her core beliefs is in sustainable harvesting and ethical foraging. She firmly believes that it is possible to enjoy the bounty of nature without causing harm to the environment or depleting its resources. In her books, she provides practical tips and advice on how to forage in a way that is both sustainable and respectful of the natural world.

Whether you are an experienced forager or a beginner looking to learn more about the plants that grow in your backyard, Shannon's books are an invaluable resource that will inspire and inform you. With her expert guidance, you, too, can discover the many benefits of wild edible plants and unlock the secrets of the natural world.

BIBLIOGRAPHY

Photo attributions

Nereocystis luetkeana (K.Mertens) Postels & Ruprecht observed in the United States of America by redrover-tracy (licensed under http://creativecommons.org/licenses/by/4.0/)

Nereocystis luetkeana (K.Mertens) Postels & Ruprecht observed in the United States of America by Daniel Gillies (licensed under http://creativecommons.org/licenses/by/4.0/)

Undaria pinnatifida (Harv.) Suringar observed in the United States of America by Cricket Raspet (licensed under http://creativecommons.org/licenses/by/4.0/)

Zostera marina L. observed in the United States of America by Evie Fachon (licensed under http://creativecommons.org/licenses/by/4.0/)

Pinus monophylla Torr. & Frém. observed in the United States of America by Marty Purdy (licensed under http://creativecommons.org/licenses/by/4.0/)

Pinus monophylla Torr. & Frém. observed in the United States of America by joergmlpts (licensed under http://creativecommons.org/licenses/by/4.0/)

Ulmus pumila L. observed in the United States of America by Brett Ortler (licensed under http://creativecommons.org/licenses/by/4.0/)

Ulmus pumila L. observed in the United States of America by Tamberly Conway (licensed under http://creativecommons.org/licenses/by/4.0/)

Ulmus pumila L. observed in the United States of America by CK Kelly (licensed under http://creativecommons.org/licenses/by/4.0/)

Rhododendron tomentosum (Stokes) Harmaja observed in the United States of America by Brooke Smith (licensed under http://creativecommons.org/licenses/by/4.0/)

https://www.desert-tropicals.com/Plants/Fabaceae/Olneya_tesota.html

Rubus parviflorus Mary Walcott 1925 licensed under https://creativecommons.org/licenses/by-sa/3.0/

Amanita ocreata observed in the United States of America by Alan Rockefeller (licensed under http://creativecommons.org/licenses/by-sa/4.0/)

Blackthorn in blossom.jpg Photo by Tom Corser www.tomcorser.com. Licensed under Creative Commons Attribution-ShareAlike 3.0 Unported Licence: https://creativecommons.org/licenses/by-sa/3.0/legalcode").

Umbellularia californica observed in the United States of America by Bri Weldon (licensed under https://creativecommons.org/licenses/by/2.0/).

References

V. A. P. B. D. P. H. (2014, March 25). *"14 Wonderful Benefits of Eating Land Cress."* Relax Into Success. https://paulhaider.wordpress.com/2014/03/25/14-wonderful-benefits-of-eating-land-cress/

A Modern Herbal | Pimpernel, Scarlet. (n.d.). https://www.botanical.com/botanical/mgmh/p/pimper33.html

Access to this page has been denied. (n.d.). https://cookpad.com/us/recipes/4043171-sauteed-black-nightshade

Adamant, A. (2021, August 17). *Foraging Yellow Dock (Curly Dock, and other Rumex sp.).* Practical Self Reliance. https://practicalselfreliance.com/foraging-yellow-dock-curly-dock-rumex-sp/

Alaska☐s Wilderness Medicines - Angelica. (n.d.). http://www.ankn.uaf.edu/curriculum/books/Viereck/viereckangelica.html

Aleuria aurantia (MushroomExpert.Com). (n.d.). http://www.mushroomexpert.com/aleuria_aurantia.html

Alfalfa: Health Benefits, Side Effects, Uses, Dose & Precautions. (2021, June 11). RxList. https://www.rxlist.com/alfalfa/supplements.htm

Alfalfa (Medicago sativa). (n.d.). https://www.illinoiswildflowers.info/weeds/plants/alfalfa.htm

Amelanchier alnifolia Saskatoon, Saskatoon serviceberry, Serviceberry PFAF Plant Database. (n.d.). https://pfaf.org/user/plant.aspx?LatinName=Amelanchier+alnifolia

Angelica lucida (sea coast Angelica): Go Botany. (n.d.). https://gobotany.nativeplanttrust.org/species/angelica/lucida/

Annual Sowthistle. (2018, June 29). College of Agricultural Sciences. https://horticulture.oregonstate.edu/weed/annual-sowthistle

Apple Brown Butter Bay Leaf Spice Cookies for the Gluten Free Ratio Rally. (2017, October 12). Eat the Love. https://www.eatthelove.com/apple-brown-butter-bay-leaf-spice-cookies/

Are berries safe for my dog to eat? (2022, August 8). Your Dog. https://www.yourdog.co.uk/dog-care-and-advice/are-berries-safe-for-my-dog-to-eat/

Are Goji Berries Safe for Dogs? Benefits and Risks - Dog Wish. (2021a, December 28). Dogwish. https://dogwish.com/nutrition/fruits/can-dogs-eat-goji-berries

Are Goji Berries Safe for Dogs? Benefits and Risks - Dog Wish. (2021b, December 28). Dogwish. https://dogwish.com/nutrition/fruits/can-dogs-eat-goji-berries

Arundo donax Giant Reed, Giant Reed Grass PFAF Plant Database. (n.d.). https://pfaf.org/User/Plant.aspx?LatinName=Arundo+donax

Atriplex canescens Grey Sage Brush, Fourwing saltbush PFAF Plant Database. (n.d.). https://pfaf.org/user/plant.aspx?latinname=Atriplex+canescens

Backyard, M. N. (2022, November 26). *Plant of the Month (May): Wooly bluecurls – Trichostema lanatum.* http://mother-natures-backyard.blogspot.com/2016/05/plant-of-month-may-wooly-bluecurls.html

Barhum, L. (2018, August 7). *What are the health benefits of goji berries?* https://www.medicalnewstoday.com/articles/322693

Bear Grass Poisoning in Dogs. (2016, July 14). Symptoms, Causes, Diagnosis, Treatment, Recovery, Management, Cost. https://wagwalking.com/condition/bear-grass-poisoning

Bear Grass, Resilient Rhizomes. (2021, November 16). Eat the Planet. https://eattheplanet.org/bear-grass-resilient-rhizomes/

Beargrass (U.S. National Park Service). (n.d.). https://www.nps.gov/articles/beargrass.htm

Bhardwaj, N. (2022, April 19). *From arthritis to period cramps, black nightshade will help you deal with it all naturally.* Healthshots. https://www.healthshots.com/healthy-eating/nutrition/5-health-benefits-of-makoy-or-black-nightshade/

BioLib Online Library of Biological Books. (n.d.). http://www.biolib.de/

Black Nightshade Berries. (n.d.). https://specialtyproduce.com/produce/Black_Nightshade_Berries_12970.php

Black Nightshade facts and health benefits. (2020, January 1). Health Benefits | Health Benefits of Foods and Drinks. https://www.healthbenefitstimes.com/black-nightshade/

Black Swamp Gooseberry, Ribes lacustre. (2016, October 3). Native Plants PNW. http://nativeplantspnw.com/black-swamp-gooseberry-ribes-lacustre/

Blackthorn. (n.d.). Dr. Hauschka. https://www.drhauschka.de/en/cosmos/values/organic-raw-materials-from-around-the-world/medicinal-plant-glossary/blackthorn/

Blackthorn facts and health benefits. (2019, February 25). Health Benefits | Health Benefits of Foods and Drinks. https://www.healthbenefitstimes.com/blackthorn-or-sloe/

Bladderpod. (n.d.). Onceuponawatershed. https://www.onceuponawatershed.org/bladderpod

Bladderpod, Peritoma arborea. (n.d.). https://calscape.org/Peritoma-arborea-(Bladderpod)

Bluebead: Pictures, Flowers, Leaves & Identification | Clintonia borealis. (n.d.). https://www.ediblewildfood.com/bluebead.aspx

Bride's Bonnet. (n.d.). ASPCA. https://www.aspca.org/pet-care/animal-poison-control/toxic-and-non-toxic-plants/brides-bonnet

Brown, A. (2022, May 27). *5 Stinging Nettle Look-Alikes.* Back Garden - Gardening Blog, Plants, Landscaping, Mushrooms. https://backgarden.org/stinging-nettle-look-alikes/

Buckner, H. (2022, April 29). *How to Harvest Angelica.* Gardener's Path. https://gardenerspath.com/plants/herbs/harvest-angelica/

Burdock and curly dock dip recipe, vegetarian, gluten-free. Like spinach and artichoke, with foraged, edible weeds. (2022, November 26). https://foragedfoodie.blogspot.com/2016/11/double-dock-dip.html

Caldwell, L. (2021, June 29). *Bull Kelp.* Coastal Interpretive Center. https://interpretivecenter.org/bull-kelp/

California Bay Laurel. (n.d.). National Wildlife Federation. https://www.nwf.org/Educational-Resources/Wildlife-Guide/Plants-and-Fungi/California-Bay-Laurel

California Copperleaf, Acalypha californica. (n.d.). https://calscape.org/loc-California/Acalypha-californica-(California-Copperleaf)?srchcr=sc63544103e1b49

California Mountain Ash, Sorbus californica. (n.d.). https://calscape.org/loc-california/Sorbus+californica+()

California Poppy. (n.d.). https://www.fs.usda.gov/wildflowers/plant-of-the-week/eschscholzia_californica.shtml

California Poppy, Eschscholzia californica. (n.d.). https://calscape.org/Eschscholzia-californica-(California-Poppy)

Can Dogs Eat Bilberries? | Benefits, Risks. (n.d.). Can Dogs Eat It. https://www.candogseatit.com/fruit-veg/bilberries

Can Dogs Eat Sloe Berries? | Health Risks. (n.d.). Can Dogs Eat It. https://www.candogseatit.com/fruit-veg/sloe-berries

Candied Flowers. (2021, May 21). The Spruce Eats. https://www.thespruceeats.com/candied-flowers-521325

Chenopodium album (Baconweed, Bacon Weed, Fat Hen, Frost-blite, Goosefoot, Lambsquarters, Pigweed, White Goosefoot) | North Carolina Extension Gardener Plant Toolbox. (n.d.). https://plants.ces.ncsu.edu/plants/chenopodium-album/

Chenopodium album (lambsquarters, white goosefoot): Go Botany. (n.d.). https://gobotany.nativeplanttrust.org/species/chenopodium/album/

Claytonia perfoliata Miner's Lettuce PFAF Plant Database. (n.d.). https://pfaf.org/user/plant.aspx?LatinName=Claytonia+perfoliata

Cleavers: Pictures, Flowers, Leaves & Identification | Galium aparine. (n.d.). https://www.ediblewildfood.com/cleavers.aspx

Common Bedstraw, Galium aparine. (n.d.). https://calscape.org/loc-California/Galium+aparine+(Common+Bedstraw)?newsearch=1

Content - Health Encyclopedia - University of Rochester Medical Center. (n.d.). https://www.urmc.rochester.edu/encyclopedia/content.aspx?contenttypeid=19

Cranberry facts and health benefits. (2018, April 8). Health Benefits | Health Benefits of Foods and Drinks. https://www.healthbenefitstimes.com/cranberry/

Crowberry. (n.d.). https://elmaskincare.com/herbs/herbs_crowberry.htm

Crowberry facts and health benefits. (2021, January 18). Health Benefits | Health Benefits of Foods and Drinks. https://www.healthbenefitstimes.com/crowberry/

Cucurbita foetidissima Buffalo Gourd, Missouri gourd PFAF Plant Database. (n.d.). https://pfaf.org/user/Plant.aspx?LatinName=Cucurbita+foetidissima

Curly dock. (n.d.). Weeds. https://www.canr.msu.edu/weeds/extension/curly-dock

Cyperus esculentus (Chufa Flatsedge, Chufa Sedge, Earth Almond, Tiger Nut, Yellow Nut-grass, Yellow Nutsedge) | North Carolina Extension Gardener Plant Toolbox. (n.d.). https://plants.ces.ncsu.edu/plants/cyperus-esculentus/

DeBella, T. (2022, April 30). *What Does Nutsedge Look Like and How Do I Get Rid of it?* Family Handyman. https://www.familyhandyman.com/article/nutsedge/

Desert Ironwood. (2020, December 29). The Wood Database. https://www.wood-database.com/desert-ironwood/

Dewberry. (n.d.). Missouri Department of Conservation. https://mdc.mo.gov/discover-nature/field-guide/dewberry

Dewberry, Rubus flagellaris Willd. (n.d.). https://www.friendsofthewildflowergarden.org/pages/plants/dewberry.html

Digitalis purpurea – PlantRight. (n.d.). https://plantright.org/watch/digitalis-purpurea/

Digitalis purpurea Profile – California Invasive Plant Council. (n.d.). https://www.cal-ipc.org/plants/profile/digitalis-purpurea-profile/

DoMyOwn. (n.d.). *The Goosegrass Identification Guide.* Copyright © 2022, DoMyOwn. https://www.domyown.com/the-goosegrass-identification-guide-a-805.html

Eastern Red Bud: Pea Pods Tree. (n.d.). Eat the Weeds and Other Things, Too. https://www.eattheweeds.com/tag/cercis-occidentalis/

Empetrum nigrum (black crowberry): Go Botany. (n.d.). https://gobotany.nativeplanttrust.org/species/empetrum/nigrum/

Empetrum nigrum Crowberry, Black crowberry, Black Crowberry PFAF Plant Database. (n.d.). https://pfaf.org/user/plant.aspx?latinname=Empetrum+nigrum

Error 404 - Not Found. (n.d.-a). http://southwestdesertflora.com/WebsiteFolders/All_Species/Cappараceae/Cleome+isomeris,+Bladderpod+Spiderflower.html

Error 404 - Not Found. (n.d.-b). http://southwestdesertflora.com/WebsiteFolders/All_Species/Acanthaceae/Justicia | californica, | Chuparosa.html

Eschscholzia californica (California Poppy) | North Carolina Extension Gardener Plant Toolbox. (n.d.). https://plants.ces.ncsu.edu/plants/eschscholzia-californica/

Ficus carica (Common Fig) | North Carolina Extension Gardener Plant Toolbox. (n.d.). https://plants.ces.ncsu.edu/plants/ficus-carica/

Ficus carica Fig, Edible fig, Fig Common PFAF Plant Database. (n.d.). https://pfaf.org/user/plant.aspx?latinname=Ficus+carica

Find Trees & Learn | University of Arizona Campus Arboretum. (n.d.). https://apps.cals.arizona.edu/arboretum/taxon.aspx?id=190

Foraging Tours and Classes in California. (2022, April 23). Eat the Planet. https://eattheplanet.org/foraging-tours-and-classes-in-california/

FS1309: Crabgrass and Goosegrass Identification and Control in Cool-Season Turfgrass for Professionals (Rutgers NJAES). (n.d.). https://njaes.rutgers.edu/fs1309/

Garden Cress: Health Benefits, Side Effects, Uses, Dose & Precautions. (2021, June 11). RxList. https://www.rxlist.com/garden_cress/supplements.htm

Giant reed facts and health benefits. (2022, June 2). Health Benefits | Health Benefits of Foods and Drinks. https://www.healthbenefitstimes.com/giant-reed/

Goji Berries Side Effects: 6 Ways They May Cause Harm. (2022, October 26). STYLECRAZE. https://www.stylecraze.com/articles/serious-side-effects-of-goji-berries/

Grant, A. (2021, January 13). *Care Of Land Cress Plants: Information And Tips For Growing Upland Cress.* Gardening Know How. https://www.gardeningknowhow.com/edible/vegetables/cress/growing-upland-cress.htm

Guy, T. M. (2022, January 18). *Laccaria amethystina: The Amethyst Deceiver Identification & Look Alikes.* Healing-Mushrooms.net. https://healing-mushrooms.net/laccaria-amethystina

Harvesting Native Gardens : The Power of Plants. (n.d.). https://powerofplants.com/2019/06/harvesting-your-native-garden-2/

HarvestWild — Guided Gathering. (n.d.). HarvestWild. https://www.harvestwild.com/guided-gathering

Hinckle, J. (2022, April 6). *Can Dogs Eat Gooseberries? Are Gooseberries Safe For Dogs?* DogTime. https://dogtime.com/dog-health/dog-food-dog-nutrition/95420-can-dogs-eat-gooseberries-safe

Hollinger, H. (2022a, October 26). *Fig Poisoning in Dogs*. Signs, Causes, Diagnosis, Treatment, Recovery, Management, Cost. https://wagwalking.com/condition/fig-poisoning

Hollinger, H. (2022b, October 31). *Stinging Nettle Poisoning in Dogs*. Symptoms, Causes, Diagnosis, Treatment, Recovery, Management, Cost. https://wagwalking.com/condition/stinging-nettle-poisoning

Instructables. (2022, May 17). *How to Wildcraft Nori, Wakame and Other Seaweed*. https://www.instructables.com/How-to-Harvest-Seaweed/

Is Dock Poisonous to Cats and Dogs? (2020, March 25). Animalpath.org. https://animalpath.org/is-dock-poisonous/

Janisse, K. (2021, March 29). *Milk Thistle for Dogs: Protecting Your Dog's Liver*. https://blog.homesalive.ca/dog-blog/milk-thistle-for-dogs

Jones, R. T. D. (2016, September 3). *Alfalfa*. Healthline. https://www.healthline.com/nutrition/alfalfa

Just a moment. . . (n.d.-a). https://www.wildflower.org/plants/result.php?id_plant=ZOMA

Just a moment. . . (n.d.-b). https://www.wildflower.org/plants/result.php?id_plant=XETE

Keithy, Z. (2022, November 15). *Can Dogs Eat Sticky Weed? [Explained]*. Dog Care Tips and Information. https://dailydogdrama.com/dog-care/can-dogs-eat-sticky-weed/

Kitchen, M. P. (2010, January 21). *Braised Chicken Thighs with Bay Leaf*. My Persian Kitchen. http://www.mypersiankitchen.com/braised-chicken-thighs-with-bay-leaf/

Knowles, E. (2018, June 5). *What is saltbush?* Gourmet Traveller. https://www.gourmettraveller.com.au/recipes/explainers/what-is-saltbush-15878

Labrador Tea | Rhododendron groenlandicum. (n.d.). https://wildadirondacks.org/adirondack-shrubs-labrador-tea-rhododendron-groenlandicum.html

Labrador Tea: An abundant local edible wild plant. (2015, October 20). Food First NL. https://www.foodfirstnl.ca/rcr-archive/2013/07/labrador-tea-an-abundant-local-edible-wild-plant

Labrador Tea: Health Benefits, Side Effects, Uses, Dose & Precautions. (2021, June 11). RxList. https://www.rxlist.com/labrador_tea/supplements.htm

Lamb's Quarters | Poisonous Plant For Pets. (n.d.). https://www.pawsdogdaycare.com/toxic-and-non-toxic-plants/lambs-quarters

Land cress facts and health benefits. (2022, August 12). Health Benefits | Health Benefits of Foods and Drinks. https://www.healthbenefitstimes.com/land-cress/

Lautanen-Raleigh, M. (2022, November 26). *Cleavers - Herb of the Week*. https://backyardpatch.blogspot.com/2012/03/cleavers-herb-of-week.html

Lombardo, L. (2020, May 17). *How to Harvest and Use Curly Dock*. The Self Sufficient HomeAcre. https://www.theselfsufficienthomeacre.com/2018/05/how-to-harvest-and-use-curly-dock.html

Lycium barbarum Goji, Box Thorn, Matrimony vine PFAF Plant Database. (n.d.). https://pfaf.org/user/plant.aspx?latinname=Lycium+barbarum

Lysimachia arvensis. (n.d.). https://ucjeps.berkeley.edu/eflora/eflora_display.php?tid=99404

Lysimachia arvensis (scarlet pimpernel): Go Botany. (n.d.). https://gobotany.nativeplanttrust.org/species/lysimachia/arvensis/

Madia sativa Chile Tarweed, Coast tarweed PFAF Plant Database. (n.d.). https://pfaf.org/user/Plant.aspx?LatinName=Madia+sativa

Malus fusca Oregon Crab, Oregon crab apple PFAF Plant Database. (n.d.). https://pfaf.org/user/Plant.aspx?LatinName=Malus+fusca

Mc'Oneal, S. (2022, October 7). *Is Monkey Grass Poisonous To Dogs?* Healthy Homemade Dog Treats. https://healthyhomemadedogtreats.com/is-monkey-grass-poisonous-to-dogs/

Medicago sativa. (n.d.). https://www.fs.usda.gov/database/feis/plants/forb/medsat/all.html

Medicago sativa Alfalfa, Yellow alfalfa PFAF Plant Database. (n.d.). https://pfaf.org/user/plant.aspx?LatinName=Medicago+sativa

medicinal herbs: CROWBERRY - Empetrum nigrum. (n.d.). http://www.naturalmedicinalherbs.net/herbs/e/empetrum-nigrum=crowberry.php

medicinal herbs: EEL GRASS - Zostera marina. (n.d.). http://www.naturalmedicinalherbs.net/herbs/z/zostera-marina=eel-grass.php

medicinal herbs: SCARLET PIMPERNEL - Anagallis arvensis. (n.d.). http://www.naturalmedicinalherbs.net/herbs/a/anagallis-arvensis=scarlet-pimpernel.php

Miner's Lettuce: How to Identify, Grow and Harvest Claytonia. (2022, January 25). Homestead and Chill. https://homesteadandchill.com/miners-lettuce-identify-grow-harvest/

Missouri Gourd, Cucurbita foetidissima. (n.d.). https://calscape.org/Cucurbita-foetidissima-(Missouri-Gourd)

Mountain Ash Berries, Rowan Berry ~ 8 Best Uses. (2022, November 8). HealthyGreenSavvy. https://www.healthygreensavvy.com/mountain-ash-berries-rowan/

Nadratowska, M. (2020, October 13). *ROWAN (Mountain ash)*. Happy Healthy Kids. https://happyhealthykidsgreen.com/rowan-mountain-ash/

Olneya tesota Calflora. (n.d.). https://www.calflora.org/app/taxon?crn=5914

Orr, E. (2021, April 25). *Curly dock: edible invasive weed*. Foraging for Wild Edibles. https://www.wildedible.com/curly-dock

Pacific Crabapple, Malus fusca. (2014, November 17). Native Plants PNW. http://nativeplantspnw.com/pacific-crabapple-malus-fusca/

Pet Poison Helpline. (2020, March 4). *Stinging Nettle Are Toxic To Pets.* https://www.petpoisonhelpline.com/poison/stinging-nettle/

Pet Poison Helpline. (2022a, July 28). *Azalea Is Toxic To Dogs.* https://www.petpoisonhelpline.com/poison/azalea/

Pet Poison Helpline. (2022b, July 28). *Azalea Is Toxic To Dogs.* https://www.petpoisonhelpline.com/poison/azalea/

Philadelphia, C. H. O. (2022, October 18). *Mushroom Foraging Warning from the Poison Control Center at Children's Hospital of Philadelphia.* https://www.prnewswire.com/news-releases/mushroom-foraging-warning-from-the-poison-control-center-at-childrens-hospital-of-philadelphia-301652483.html

Pickled Bull Kelp Recipe - Food.com. (2008, November 2). https://www.food.com/recipe/pickled-bull-kelp-334435

Prickly Currant, Ribes lacustre. (n.d.). https://calscape.org/Ribes-lacustre-+()

Provings - School of Homeopathy - Goosegrass (Galium Aparine). (n.d.). https://www.homeopathyschool.com/the-school/provings/goosegrass/

Prunus spinosa Sloe - Blackthorn PFAF Plant Database. (n.d.). https://pfaf.org/user/Plant.aspx?LatinName=Prunus+spinosa

Rabins, I. (2022, March 13). *Bullwhip Kelp.* Book Wild Food Foraging Classes Online | ForageSF. https://www.foragesf.com/blog/2019/1/22/bullwhip-kelp-the-seaweed-you-can-pickle

Redbud, a Bold and Beautiful Tree with Edible Flowers. (2020, April 14). Eat the Planet. https://eattheplanet.org/redbud-a-bold-and-beautiful-tree-with-edible-flowers/

Reindeer Moss. (2017, October 24). Eat the Weeds and Other Things, Too. https://www.eattheweeds.com/edible-cladonia-whats-not-to-lichen-2/

Reindeer moss - edible wild plant - how to find, identify, prepare, and other uses for survival. -. (2019, June 3). Wilderness Arena. https://www.wildernessarena.com/food-water-shelter/food-food-water-shelter/food-procurement/edible-wild-plants/reindeer-moss

Ribes lacustre. (n.d.). https://www.wnps.org/native-plant-directory/339:ribes-lacustre

Ribes lacustre (bristly swamp currant): Go Botany. (n.d.). https://gobotany.nativeplanttrust.org/species/ribes/lacustre/

Ribes lacustre Prickly Blackcurrant, Prickly currant PFAF Plant Database. (n.d.). https://pfaf.org/user/Plant.aspx?LatinName=Ribes+lacustre

Richards, L. (2018, August 17). *Medicinal and Edible California Natives.* If Nature Could Talk. https://ifnaturecouldtalk.com/medicinal-and-edible-california-natives

Rubus flagellaris (Blackberry, Common Dewberry, Dewberry, Northern Blackberry, Northern Dewberry) | North Carolina Extension Gardener Plant Toolbox. (n.d.). https://plants.ces.ncsu.edu/plants/rubus-flagellaris/

Rubus flagellaris (northern blackberry, northern dewberry): Go Botany. (n.d.). https://gobotany.nativeplanttrust.org/species/rubus/flagellaris/

Rubus flagellaris Northern Dewberry PFAF Plant Database. (n.d.). https://pfaf.org/user/Plant.aspx?LatinName=Rubus+flagellaris

Sea-watch • Angelica lucida. (n.d.). Biodiversity of the Central Coast. https://www.centralcoastbiodiversity.org/sea-watch-bull-angelica-lucida.html

Seep Monkey Flower, Erythranthe guttata. (n.d.). https://calscape.org/loc-California/Erythranthe-guttata-(Seep-Monkey-Flower)?srchcr=sc632ca562a9c2b

SEINet Portal Network - Justicia californica. (n.d.). https://swbiodiversity.org/seinet/taxa/index.php?taxon=2568

Sherpa, S. (2016, July 28). *How to Harvest, Prepare, and Use Yellow Dock Root Medicinally.* Survival Sherpa. https://survivalsherpa.wordpress.com/2016/07/27/how-to-harvest-prepare-and-use-yellow-dock-root-medicinally/

SIMoN :: Species Database. (n.d.-a). https://sanctuarysimon.org/dbtools/species-database/id/75/nereocystis/luetkeana/bull-kelp

SIMoN :: Species Database. (n.d.-b). https://sanctuarysimon.org/dbtools/species-database/id/72/zostera/marina/eel-grass

Solanum nigrum (Blackberry Nightshade, Black Nightshade, Common Nightshade, European Black Nightshade, Garden Nightshade, Poisonberry) | North Carolina Extension Gardener Plant Toolbox. (n.d.). https://plants.ces.ncsu.edu/plants/solanum-nigrum/

Species: Atriplex canescens. (n.d.). https://www.fs.usda.gov/database/feis/plants/shrub/atrcan/all.html

Stark, E. (2021, April 25). *Pacific Northwest Native Plant Profile: Bear Grass (Xerophyllum tenax).* Real Gardens Grow Natives. https://realgardensgrownatives.com/?p=1080

Stewart, J. (2018, December 8). *Native Plant of the Month: Labrador Tea.* SHADOW. https://shadowhabitat.org/native-plant-of-the-month-labrador-tea/

Stinging nettle. (n.d.). Mount Sinai Health System. https://www.mountsinai.org/health-library/herb/stinging-nettle

The Editors of Encyclopaedia Britannica. (1998, July 20). *Bilberry | Description, Uses, & Facts.* Encyclopedia Britannica. https://www.britannica.com/plant/bilberry

The Editors of Encyclopaedia Britannica. (2022, September 29). *Fig | Description, History, Cultivation, & Types*. Encyclopedia Britannica. https://www.britannica.com/plant/fig

The FOURnet Information Network. (2010, October 24). *Crab-Apple Hot Pepper Jelly - Recipe - Cooks.com*. https://www.cooks.com/recipe/xr4ni8lt/crab-apple-hot-pepper-jelly.html

The Importance of Eelgrass. (n.d.). NOAA. https://www.fisheries.noaa.gov/feature-story/importance-eelgrass

Tokic, A. (2017, February 15). *Benefits of Kelp for Dogs*. The Honest Kitchen. https://www.thehonestkitchen.com/blogs/pet-food-ingredients/benefits-of-kelp-for-dogs

Trees for Life. (2022, May 5). *Rowan tree mythology and folklore*. https://treesforlife.org.uk/into-the-forest/trees-plants-animals/trees/rowan/rowan-mythology-and-folklore/

Trichostema lanatum. (n.d.). https://ucjeps.berkeley.edu/eflora/eflora_display.php?tid=46990

Trichostema lanceolatum-Vinegarweed. (2022, November 16). Klamath Siskiyou Native Seeds. https://klamathsiskiyouseeds.com/product/trichostema-lanceolatum-vinegarweed/

Trust, W. (n.d.). *Blackthorn (Prunus spinosa) - British Trees*. Woodland Trust. https://www.woodlandtrust.org.uk/trees-woods-and-wildlife/british-trees/a-z-of-british-trees/blackthorn/

Umbellularia californica Calflora. (n.d.). https://www.calflora.org/app/taxon?crn=8183

Umbellularia californica (California bay, California Laurel, California-laurel, Myrtle-wood, Oregon-myrtle, Pacific-myrtle, Pepperwood, Spice-tree) | North Carolina Extension Gardener Plant Toolbox. (n.d.). https://plants.ces.ncsu.edu/plants/umbellularia-californica/

Urtica dioica (Common Nettle, Stinging Nettle) | North Carolina Extension Gardener Plant Toolbox. (n.d.). https://plants.ces.ncsu.edu/plants/urtica-dioica/

Urtica dioica Stinging Nettle, California nettle PFAF Plant Database. (n.d.). https://pfaf.org/user/plant.aspx?latinname=Urtica+dioica

Vaccinium myrtillus. (n.d.). https://www.fs.usda.gov/database/feis/plants/shrub/vacmyr/all.html

Vaccinium myrtillus. (2012, January 16). The Naturopathic Herbalist. https://thenaturopathicherbalist.com/herbs/v-z/vaccinium-myrtillusblueberry/

Vaccinium oxycoccos. (n.d.). https://www.wnps.org/native-plant-directory/49:vaccinium-oxycoccos

Vaccinium oxycoccos Small Cranberry PFAF Plant Database. (n.d.). https://pfaf.org/user/Plant.aspx?LatinName=Vaccinium+oxycoccos

Veda, V. (2021, June 28). *Ayurveda Nightshades | Kakamachi (Solanum Nigrum) Uses & Jam Recipe*. Vital Veda. https://vitalveda.com.au/learn/kakamachi/

W., M. (2019, March 22). *Identifying Lamb's Quarters*. Four Season Foraging. https://www.fourseasonforaging.com/blog/2017/7/2/identifying-lambs-quarters

W., M. (2020, February 3). *Curly Dock: A Plant for Year-Round Sustenance*. Four Season Foraging. https://www.fourseasonforaging.com/blog/2020/1/25/curly-dock

Weed Gallery: Annual sowthistle-UC IPM. (n.d.). http://ipm.ucanr.edu/PMG/WEEDS/annual_sowthistle.html

Weed Gallery: Black nightshade-UC IPM. (n.d.). http://ipm.ucanr.edu/PMG/WEEDS/black_nightshade.html

Weed Gallery: Common lambsquarters--UC IPM. (n.d.). http://ipm.ucanr.edu/PMG/WEEDS/lambsquarters.html

Weed Gallery: Yellow nutsedge--UC IPM. (n.d.). http://ipm.ucanr.edu/PMG/WEEDS/yellow_nutsedge.html

Western Redbud, Cercis occidentalis. (n.d.). https://calscape.org/Cercis-occidentalis-(Western-Redbud)

Western Serviceberry - Amelanchier alnifolia - PNW Plants. (n.d.). Copyright (C) 2006 Filaret Ilas. All Rights Reserved. http://www.pnwplants.wsu.edu/PlantDisplay.aspx?PlantID=345

Western Serviceberry, Amelanchier alnifolia. (n.d.). https://calscape.org/Amelanchier-alnifolia-+()

Wikipedia contributors. (2021a, August 23). *Sorbus californica*. Wikipedia. https://en.wikipedia.org/wiki/Sorbus_californica

Wikipedia contributors. (2021b, September 29). *Clintonia uniflora*. Wikipedia. https://en.wikipedia.org/wiki/Clintonia_uniflora

Wikipedia contributors. (2022a, January 22). *Rubus flagellaris*. Wikipedia. https://en.wikipedia.org/wiki/Rubus_flagellaris

Wikipedia contributors. (2022b, June 12). *Sonchus oleraceus*. Wikipedia. https://en.wikipedia.org/wiki/Sonchus_oleraceus

Wikipedia contributors. (2022c, June 16). *Empetrum nigrum*. Wikipedia. https://en.wikipedia.org/wiki/Empetrum_nigrum

Wikipedia contributors. (2022d, June 21). *Lycium barbarum*. Wikipedia. https://en.wikipedia.org/wiki/Lycium_barbarum

Wikipedia contributors. (2022e, June 24). *Atriplex canescens*. Wikipedia. https://en.wikipedia.org/wiki/Atriplex_canescens

Wikipedia contributors. (2022f, June 24). *Cercis occidentalis*. Wikipedia. https://en.wikipedia.org/wiki/Cercis_occidentalis

Wikipedia contributors. (2022g, June 24). *Justicia californica*. Wikipedia. https://en.wikipedia.org/wiki/Justicia_californica

Wikipedia contributors. (2022h, June 24). *Madia sativa*. Wikipedia. https://en.wikipedia.org/wiki/Madia_sativa

Wikipedia contributors. (2022i, August 16). *Xerophyllum tenax*. Wikipedia. https://en.wikipedia.org/wiki/Xerophyllum_tenax

Wikipedia contributors. (2022j, August 21). *Nereocystis*. Wikipedia. https://en.wikipedia.org/wiki/Nereocystis

Wikipedia contributors. (2022k, August 25). *Vaccinium oxycoccos*. Wikipedia. https://en.wikipedia.org/wiki/Vaccinium_oxycoccos

Wikipedia contributors. (2022l, August 29). *Claytonia perfoliata*. Wikipedia. https://en.wikipedia.org/wiki/Claytonia_perfoliata

Wikipedia contributors. (2022m, September 1). *Olneya*. Wikipedia. https://en.wikipedia.org/wiki/Olneya

Wikipedia contributors. (2022n, September 7). *Rowan*. Wikipedia. https://en.wikipedia.org/wiki/Rowan

Wikipedia contributors. (2022o, September 30). *Amelanchier alnifolia*. Wikipedia. https://en.wikipedia.org/wiki/Amelanchier_alnifolia

Wikipedia contributors. (2022p, October 2). *Zostera marina*. Wikipedia. https://en.wikipedia.org/wiki/Zostera_marina

Wikipedia contributors. (2022q, October 11). *Aconitum napellus*. Wikipedia. https://en.wikipedia.org/wiki/Aconitum_napellus

Wikipedia contributors. (2022r, October 12). *Cladonia rangiferina*. Wikipedia. https://en.wikipedia.org/wiki/Cladonia_rangiferina

Wikipedia contributors. (2022s, October 13). *Arundo donax*. Wikipedia. https://en.wikipedia.org/wiki/Arundo_donax

Wikipedia contributors. (2022t, October 18). *Vaccinium myrtillus*. Wikipedia. https://en.wikipedia.org/wiki/Vaccinium_myrtillus

Wikipedia contributors. (2022u, October 19). *Wakame*. Wikipedia. https://en.wikipedia.org/wiki/Wakame

Wikipedia contributors. (2022v, October 20). *Eschscholzia californica*. Wikipedia. https://en.wikipedia.org/wiki/Eschscholzia_californica

Wikipedia contributors. (2022w, October 26). *Alfalfa*. Wikipedia. https://en.wikipedia.org/wiki/Alfalfa

Wikipedia contributors. (2022x, October 26). *Umbellularia*. Wikipedia. https://en.wikipedia.org/wiki/Umbellularia

Wikipedia contributors. (2022y, November 3). *Malus fusca*. Wikipedia. https://en.wikipedia.org/wiki/Malus_fusca

Wikipedia contributors. (2022z, November 16). *Cucurbita foetidissima*. Wikipedia. https://en.wikipedia.org/wiki/Cucurbita_foetidissima

Wikipedia contributors. (2022aa, November 19). *Chenopodium album*. Wikipedia. https://en.wikipedia.org/wiki/Chenopodium_album

Wikipedia contributors. (2022ab, November 22). *Fig*. Wikipedia. https://en.wikipedia.org/wiki/Fig

Wikipedia contributors. (2022ac, November 24). *Galium aparine*. Wikipedia. https://en.wikipedia.org/wiki/Galium_aparine

Wikipedia contributors. (2022ad, November 24). *Prunus spinosa*. Wikipedia. https://en.wikipedia.org/wiki/Prunus_spinosa

Wikipedia contributors. (2022ae, November 24). *Urtica dioica*. Wikipedia. https://en.wikipedia.org/wiki/Urtica_dioica

Wikipedia contributors. (2022af, November 25). *Cyperus esculentus*. Wikipedia. https://en.wikipedia.org/wiki/Cyperus_esculentus

Wild Mushroom Warning. (n.d.). https://www.poison.org/articles/wild-mushroom-warning

Wilson, B., & Wilson, C. (n.d.). *Atriplex canescens, Four-wing Salt Bush*. https://www.laspilitas.com/nature-of-california/plants/103--atriplex-canescens

Witch in the Woods Botanicals. (n.d.). *CALIFORNIA POPPY*. Witch in the Woods Botanicals. https://witchinthewoodsbotanicals.com/pages/california-poppy

Woolly Bluecurls, Trichostema lanatum. (n.d.). https://calscape.org/Trichostema-lanatum-(Woolly-Bluecurls)

Written by: Madalene. (2015, March 19). *Gooseberry and Bay Leaf Jam*. The British Larder. https://britishlarder.co.uk/gooseberry-and-bay-leaf-jam/

Xerophyllum tenax Indian Basket Grass, Common beargrass PFAF Plant Database. (n.d.). https://pfaf.org/User/Plant.aspx?LatinName=Xerophyllum+tenax

Yan, P. (2022, November 12). *How to Identify Wild Cranberry (Vaccinium oxycoccos)*. Eco Friendly Income. https://www.ecofriendlyincome.com/blog/how-to-identify-wild-cranberry